SECURITY IN NORTH AFRICA
Internal and External Challenges

Ian O. Lesser

Prepared for the
United States Air Force

RAND

Project AIR FORCE

The emotional reaction across North Africa during the Gulf War, and the deepening turmoil in Algeria as the country grapples with an assertive Islamic movement, have awakened Western interest in the prospects for stability along the southern shore of the Mediterranean. The alarming demographic imbalance between north and south and the resulting flow of migrants to an increasingly inhospitable Europe is now a feature of the European security debate. To these concerns must be added the risk of nuclear and ballistic missile proliferation emanating from Libya and Algeria. Among foreign and security policy elites and publics in southern Europe, France, and to a growing degree in Europe as a whole, it has become fashionable to refer to a new "arc of crisis" in the south.

Previous RAND reports have charted this new aspect of the European security environment and the significance for U.S. policy.[1] The North African dimension of the evolving security situation in the Mediterranean was not systematically explored in these reports, except as it was reflected in the views of southern Europeans. This report attempts to fill this gap, focusing on regional developments as seen from the south. The report discusses the prospects for stability in Morocco, Algeria, and Tunisia, identifies regional flashpoints, and assesses the implications for U.S. policy. Particular attention is devoted to the outlook for regional integration (the Arab Maghreb

---

[1]See Ian O. Lesser, *Mediterranean Security: New Perspectives and Implications for U.S. Policy,* RAND, R-4178-AF, 1992.

Union) and the proliferation of weapons of mass destruction as two paths in the search for strategic weight after the Cold War.

This research, including conversations with leading officials and observers in the region, was completed in June 1992 and was conducted within the Strategy and Doctrine Program of Project AIR FORCE (a federally funded research and development center at RAND). This and other research on Mediterranean security issues form an important part of a project entitled "European Security in the Post-Cold War World," sponsored by the United States Air Force, Europe (USAFE) and the Air Staff (AF/XOXXE).

CONTENTS

SUMMARY

The emotional reaction across North Africa during the Gulf crisis, coupled with the turmoil and potential for an Islamic takeover in Algeria, have drawn attention to the importance of developments along the southern shore of the Mediterranean for security on the European periphery. The alarming demographic imbalance between a "rich" Europe and a "poor" and increasingly populous North Africa, and the resulting migration pressure, have become prominent issues in the new European security debate. Taken together with the risk of nuclear and ballistic missile proliferation emanating from Libya and Algeria, it is not surprising that some Europeans refer to a "threat from the south" and view the Mediterranean region as a whole as Europe's new "arc of crisis."

The United States has been a power in the western Mediterranean and has had a role in North African affairs for almost 200 years. Much of the current pattern of political-military involvement in the region is a product of the Cold War. But emerging security and security-related problems will compel the attention of policymakers concerned with maintaining a relevant U.S. involvement in European and Mediterranean security. From the U.S. perspective, the strategic importance of the Maghreb—Mauritania, Morocco, Algeria, Tunisia, and Libya—derives from its role as an extension of the new European security environment, its political and logistical connection to areas of importance beyond the Mediterranean basin (the Persian Gulf, sub-Saharan Africa), and its character as a center of regional risks.

Trends in the key Maghreb countries—Morocco, Algeria, and Tunisia, will have an important bearing on the prospects for north-south relations in security terms. The environment for the United States as air and naval power, and as a political actor in the region, will be shaped by security perceptions and strategic cultures from Rabat to Tunis, in addition to the more familiar views of southern Europeans.

REGIONAL TRENDS

The primacy of internal security. For Morocco, Algeria, and Tunisia, security is above all a matter of domestic stability. The growing strength of Islamic opposition movements across the region, together with growing pressure for democratization, have brought internal challenges to the forefront. All three countries face massive demographic and economic problems of a long-term nature. European restrictions on immigration, coupled with competing aid and investment priorities in Eastern Europe and the former Soviet Union, worsen the outlook for development and stability. Many of the "external" threats to the security of states in the region are actually based on the perceived vulnerability of regimes to externally inspired rebellion.

Militant Islam poses an immediate political challenge, with significant security implications. The advent of radical Islamic regimes in North Africa would have important security consequences, not least because of the unpredictable interaction with migration and proliferation issues. But the emergence of an Islamic government through democratic means in Algeria or elsewhere need not have the same implications for security as the triumph of extremists through violent struggle. A principal risk from the Western perspective is that Islamic opposition, having been driven underground, will develop a more extreme and internationalist character.

North Africans fear a post-Cold War confrontation along north-south lines. The rise of the xenophobic, anti-immigrant right in Europe and the debate over the "threat from the south" in moderate foreign and security policy circles in the West as a whole have fueled concerns that a new post-Cold War ideological struggle is developing between north and south, and in particular, between Islam and the West. A functioning European defense capability is viewed with alarm because of its presumed orientation toward "out-of-area" risks, especially those emanating from the south.

The region as a whole will be characterized by a search for geostrategic weight after the Cold War. Old rationales for strategic attention based on the geography of containment (e.g., the location of Morocco and Tunisia at key Mediterranean "choke points"), or the ability to play one superpower against the other, have lost their relevance. For Algiers and Tunis, the nonaligned movement can no longer serve as an effective vehicle for international activism and national prestige. All three countries must embark on a new search for geostrategic weight as a basis for being "taken seriously," regionally and internationally. Alternative means of acquiring greater weight include regional integration (the Arab Maghreb Union), closer relations with Europe or the United States, territorial extension, and the acquisition of weapons of mass destruction. Algeria, Morocco and Tunisia share a tradition of diplomatic mediation that may also serve as a vehicle for prestige and influence.

Incentives for proliferation are high; interest in arms control is low. During the Cold War, Algeria and Tunisia had been among the leading advocates of force reductions in the Mediterranean as a means of reducing the military presence of the superpowers. In the wake of the Gulf War and the collapse of the Soviet Union, these countries now argue for the right of North African states to acquire the means of self defense, including nuclear, chemical, ballistic missile, and submarine technology, unconstrained by arms control regimes. The incentives for proliferation, or "virtual" proliferation (e.g., the Algerian nuclear program), are high in an era of diminished superpower constraints on the behavior of regional actors. In broader terms, nuclear and ballistic missile programs are a potent source of strategic weight.

Foreign and security policies across the region are shaped by the tension between public and elite opinion, with important implications for crisis behavior. The Gulf War pointed to the ability of popular opinion to overwhelm the pro-Western inclinations of moderate regimes in Rabat and Tunis.

Leading flashpoints in the region are largely, but not exclusively, south-south. These include competition and the risk of territorial conflict between Algeria and Morocco, Libyan aggression against Tunisia, a Moroccan or Tunisian clash with Algeria over attempts to export Islamic revolution, and renewed conflict in the western Sahara, with or without Algerian or Libyan intervention. Only in the case of a Libyan or Algerian attack on Tunisia would there be a high probability of Western involvement.

Less likely, but with more serious consequences for European and U.S. security interests, are the following north-south contingencies: A ballistic missile, nuclear, or chemical threat to European territory from Libya or Algeria; a Moroccan move against the Spanish enclaves of Ceuta and Melilla; an Algerian or Libyan attack on Western ships or aircraft, perhaps against the background of a major Middle Eastern or North African crisis; and a regionally inspired terrorist incident or hostage crisis. All might lead to a preemptive or retaliatory strike by U.S. or European forces.

IMPLICATIONS FOR U.S. POLICY

• *Algeria is likely to emerge as the leading regional actor from the U.S. perspective.* Regardless of Algeria's political evolution, the country's size, energy resources, penchant for international activism, military potential, and nuclear ambitions are likely to make it the leading actor in the region. Policy toward Algeria is likely to play a far more prominent role in future U.S. policy toward the region as a whole. Algeria is already an important test case for our ability to reconcile conflicting attitudes toward democracy and radical Islam. Longer-term U.S. interests in the stable evolution of the region will be best served by a restoration of the democratic process, including the participation of Islamic parties. Closer relations with Algeria, including future economic and security assistance initiatives, should be predicated on progress in this direction.

• *A high-profile presence or significantly expanded security cooperation with the Maghreb countries is undesirable.* Morocco, Tunisia, and Algeria are keen to develop closer political, economic, and security assistance ties with Washington. Expanded political and commercial ties would be beneficial. Only Morocco has expressed a consistent interest in more active security cooperation and the provision of military facilities. In the wake of the

Gulf War and its effect in North Africa, greatly expanded defense cooperation is inadvisable and probably impossible in any case. A U.S. presence would pose unacceptable risks for little strategic benefit and could undermine the political legitimacy of existing regimes.

- *With limited exceptions, the prospects for cooperation and access to facilities in times of crisis are poor.* Again, in the wake of the Gulf experience, the prospects for access to bases and the provision of overflight rights must be considered poor, with the exception of direct threats to Moroccan and Tunisian territory. Even in the unlikely event that cooperation is offered, the use of regional facilities to support operations elsewhere in the Arab world could have negative consequences for stability in the host country and in North Africa as a whole.

- *The proliferation of weapons of mass destruction and the means for their delivery at longer range will have a profound effect on security in southern Europe and will influence the prospects for U.S. access in periods of crisis.* The ability of Algeria or Libya to hold at risk population centers and military facilities in southern Europe would exert a powerful influence on crisis decisionmaking from Lisbon to Athens. It is possible that within the next ten years, every southern European capitol will be within range of ballistic missiles based in North Africa. Under these conditions, southern European allies will expect a substantial measure of residual U.S. presence in the Mediterranean for the purposes of deterrence and reassurance in the context of cooperation in crises outside the NATO area.

- *The U.S. presence in and around the Mediterranean enjoys substantial support in Morocco and Tunisia. Even in Algiers, the U.S. presence is regarded as a potentially useful counterbalance to Europe.* As the countries of North Africa worry about the future of relations with Europe on a variety of fronts, from immigration to security, improved relations with the United States loom as an attractive hedge in political, economic, and strategic terms. In Rabat and Tunis, the U.S. military presence in the region is seen as a critical contribution to security in a more dangerous post-Cold War environment.

ACKNOWLEDGMENTS

I wish to thank the many individuals in Rabat, Tunis, and Algiers who kindly agreed to be interviewed as part of this research. I am also indebted to RAND colleagues Joseph Kechichian, David Ochmanek, Christopher Bowie, Graham Fuller, and Patricia Bedrosian, and John Chipman of the International Institute for Strategic Studies in London, for their valuable comments and assistance. Any errors or omissions are of course my own.

Chapter One

INTRODUCTION

In some ways, the three leading countries of the Maghreb—Morocco, Algeria, and Tunisia—have been profoundly affected by the recent changes on the international scene. In other ways, they have hardly been touched at all. In terms of strategic importance and regional security concerns, the demise of the East-West competition has brought radical change to all three countries. To the extent that security agendas across the region continue to be dominated by questions of domestic stability, very little has changed, although the substance and severity of these internal challenges have evolved considerably since the end of the Cold War.

This report is concerned with the internal and external challenges facing Morocco, Algeria, and Tunisia and the place of these countries in the broader Mediterranean security environment. Throughout, the analysis is concerned with the importance of the Maghreb in U.S. strategic planning and seeks to identify regional flashpoints and their implications for U.S. policy. The study takes as its starting point the thesis that the Mediterranean will continue to be important to the United States after the Cold War, first, as an extension of the European security environment at a time when Europeans are increasingly concerned about a perceived "threat from the south" and the future of the U.S. presence in and around the continent. Second, the Mediterranean will continue to function, politically and logistically, as "the place where the Persian Gulf begins," an anteroom to the security environment in the Middle East and Southwest Asia. Finally, the Mediterranean and its subregions will be areas of strategic consequence in their own right beyond the East-West competition. The strategic importance of the Maghreb—Mauritania, Morocco, Algeria, Tunisia, and Libya—derives from all three sources.

Although the study treats trends across the Maghreb and their implications, the focus is overwhelmingly on developments in Morocco, Algeria, and Tunisia. There are several reasons for this. First, these are countries where the United States either has had, or could well have, a substantial political-military presence. Morocco was accorded considerable regional importance in U.S. policy throughout the Cold War. Even in the absence of Cold War imperatives, Morocco's involvement in issues of concern to the European Community (EC), continuing entanglement in the Western Sahara dispute, and active role in Middle Eastern affairs will command the attention of policymakers. Algeria's size, energy resources, tradition of international activism, and nuclear aspirations alone would give Algiers a leading place in the regional security picture. Taken together with the deepening political crisis in Algiers and the very real possibility of an Islamic triumph, these factors place Algeria at center stage. Tunisia bears examination for somewhat different reasons. Small and relatively prosperous, Tunisia has well-developed political, economic, and security ties with the EC and the United States. Tunisia also faces a strong Islamic protest movement and adopted an overtly pro-Iraqi stance during the Gulf War. With a Libyan threat to its territory looming in the background and a very modest capacity for self defense, Tunisia is a leading "consumer" of security in regional terms, with important implications for bilateral relations with the United States. All three countries are exploring diplomatic and military initiatives aimed at bolstering their strategic weight after the Cold War.

Developments in Libya, and Libyan perceptions of their country's role in Mediterranean security, are not explicitly addressed in this study, although the regional consequences of potential Libyan actions are explored. The closed and highly unpredictable character of the Libyan regime makes analysis of the Libyan domestic scene the deserved province of specialists. In any case, Libya is very much an actor on the periphery of the Maghrebi security environment, whereas Morocco, Algeria, and Tunisia are at the core. For similar reasons, I have chosen to avoid a detailed discussion of the situation in Mauritania. In general terms, the analysis is concerned with the security situation in the western Mediterranean as seen from the

Maghreb—developments further afield, for example in Egypt or the Sudan, are not addressed.

Chapter Two

A NEW STRATEGIC LANDSCAPE

ORIGINS OF THE U.S. ROLE

The current pattern of U.S. political-military presence and interest in the Maghreb is in large measure a residue of the Cold War and the strategy of containment. Europeans and Maghrebis are also aware of a much older history of American involvement in the region. Indeed, the United States has been a power in the western Mediterranean for almost 200 years, beginning with efforts to suppress the Barbary pirates and the arrival of a U.S. naval squadron off Gibraltar in 1801.[1] Morocco was the first foreign state to recognize the United States, and Washington has maintained diplomatic representation in Morocco, Algeria, and Tunisia since the late eighteenth century.[2] With the conclusion of the anti-piracy operations against Algiers, with whom a treaty was concluded in 1815, the U.S. naval and commercial presence began to spread eastward across the Mediterranean to the Levant. But the American presence off the North African shore remained and was supported by access to the large naval base at Port Mahon in the Ballearic Islands.[3]

---

[1]In the context of the long history of piracy in the region, the United States arrived on the scene very late. Some flavor of the predations endured by European commerce at the hands of North African corsairs can be found in C. R. Pennell (ed.), *Piracy and Diplomacy in Seventeenth Century North Africa* (London: Associated University Presses, 1989).

[2]See Richard B. Parker, *North Africa: Regional Tensions and Strategic Concerns* (New York: Praeger, 1984), pp. 141–142.

[3]The early history of the United States in the region is surveyed in James A. Field, *America and the Mediterranean World, 1776–1882* (Princeton: Princeton University

Maghrebis (and the French) also recall the generally sympathetic attitude of the United States to Algerian, Moroccan, and Tunisian independence movements at the close of the colonial era. Washington was very reluctant to recognize the French protectorate over Morocco. In fact it was the last major power to do so. Washington's willingness to hold discussions with local as well as colonial administrations during the 1940s continued a tradition that can be traced onward through the Kennedy administration's open support of Algerian independence.[4] This early history of support provides a positive background for the current reassessment of bilateral relations across the region and figures prominently in the views of local officials and observers.

Modern U.S. strategic interest in the region began in earnest with the large-scale operations in North Africa during World War II. The Operation Torch landings in Morocco and the subsequent campaign in Tunisia led to the establishment of a substantial U.S. air and naval presence from Morocco to Libya. In grand strategic terms, the control of North Africa was important to safeguard Allied communications through the Mediterranean—a key link in the logistic chain from North America, across the Atlantic to the European periphery and beyond to Suez, the Persian Gulf, and the British Empire in Asia. No less important was North Africa's role as a base for attacking the German and Italian position in southern Europe and, ultimately, as a springboard for offensive action in Italy and France. In 1942 and 1943, North Africa was also of considerable importance as a theater in which something could be done at a time when the scope for offensive action was limited.[5] An essential aspect of this experience, one that would be reinforced after 1945 and continues to shape U.S. interest in the region, concerns the definition of North Africa's strategic significance in terms of its effect, first, on European security, and, second, on access to areas beyond the Mediterranean littoral in the Middle East.

Press, 1969). See also Frank Gervasi, *Thunder over the Mediterranean* (New York: David McKay, 1975).

[4]Parker, *op. cit.*, p. 142.

[5]See Michael Howard, *The Mediterranean Strategy in the Second World War* (London: Weidenfeld and Nicholson, 1968).

THE COLD WAR LEGACY

The World War II campaigns in North Africa left the United States with postwar access to a string of bases in the Maghreb. The French naval base at port Lyautey (later renamed Kenitra) north of Rabat evolved into an important communications facility for the Sixth Fleet, in use in some form until 1978. Above all, the United States developed three Strategic Air Command (SAC) bases in Morocco— Sidi Slimane, Nouasseur, and Ben Guerir—in addition to the very active range facilities at Wheelus Air Force Base in Libya. In the late 1940s and 1950s, access to air bases in North Africa played a critical role in strategic planning for the attack of the Soviet position in Eurasia, under circumstances in which the maintenance of useful bases on the European continent was open to doubt.[6]

Over four decades, U.S. interest in the stability of North Africa was closely tied to the perceived importance of events in the region to the broader East-West strategic competition. As the Soviet Union increased its naval presence and capability in the Mediterranean, in particular its large increase in activity between and after the Middle East wars of 1967 and 1973, U.S. planners became increasingly concerned about the Soviet threat to NATO's lines of communication in the Mediterranean.[7] This concern focused above all on key choke points—the Turkish Straits, Suez, and Gibraltar. As the nuclear stalemate hardened and strategists began to consider the possibility of a conventional NATO-Warsaw Pact conflict of longer rather than shorter duration, the Soviet ability to conduct a campaign of maritime interdiction—a traditional *guerre de course*—became an increasingly troubling issue. The prospect of Soviet access to bases in the western Mediterranean, on the pattern of facilities available in Egypt (at least until 1973) and Syria, troubled Western observers, as

---

[6]The role of North Africa in postwar strategic planning is addressed in Melvyn P. Leffler, *A Preponderance of Power: National Security, the Truman Administration and the Cold War* (Stanford: Stanford University Press, 1992), pp. 226–229.

[7]See Stansfield Turner, "The Future of the U.S. Navy in the Mediterranean," *Mediterranean Quarterly*, Vol. 3, No. 1, Winter 1992. See also, Michael McGwire, "Soviet Strategic Aims and Capabilities in the Mediterranean, Part I"; and Gordon McCormick, "Soviet Strategic Aims and Capabilities in the Mediterranean, Part II," in *Prospects for Security in the Mediterranean* (Adelphi Paper No. 229, London: International Institute for Strategic Studies, 1988).

did the stockpiling of large quantities of modern Soviet hardware in Libya throughout the late 1970s and early 1980s.[8]

In the Cold War context, Morocco was reasonably portrayed as a Western bulwark at a critical maritime crossroad, a consideration that loomed particularly large prior to the Spanish entry into NATO. Algeria, a leading member of the nonaligned movement, with considerable political and military-industrial ties to the Soviet Union and Eastern Europe, was held at arm's length. Libya, in the last decade of the Cold War, was seen as an unpredictable radical state, a likely springboard for Soviet activity in North Africa in the event of conflict, and a source of international terrorism aimed at U.S. and European targets. In the mid-1980s, there were several air clashes in a protracted confrontation with Libya over freedom of navigation in the Gulf of Sidra, culminating in the April 1986 El Dorado Canyon operations against Tripoli and Benghazi in retaliation for Colonel Qaddafi's sponsorship of terrorist attacks in Europe. These activities, and the unsuccessful Libyan ballistic missile attack against the LORAN station at Lampedusa in 1986, marked a general shift in European and U.S. concerns from the threat posed by Soviet power in the Mediterranean to risks emanating from regional actors.

With the decline of Soviet naval activity in the Mediterranean in the late 1980s, the winding-down of the East-West competition, and, finally, the disintegration of the Soviet Union itself, the strategic underpinnings of U.S. policy toward the western Mediterranean and the Maghreb have been removed. The Mediterranean retains its strategic significance in the broadest sense for the reasons referred to above—relevance to the European security environment, proximity to the Gulf, and a concentration of potential flashpoints—but the importance of individual Maghrebi states in geostrategic terms is now an entirely open question.[9]   For example, it is unclear that

---

[8]The details and implications of Libya's stockpiled arsenal are discussed in Maurizio Cremasco, "Two Uncertain Futures: Libya and Tunisia," in *Prospects for Security in the Mediterranean, Part III* (Adelphi Paper No. 231, London: IISS, 1988), pp. 50–54.

[9]The evolving strategic significance of the Mediterranean and implications for U.S. policy are addressed in detail in Ian O. Lesser, *Mediterranean Security: New Perspectives and Implications for U.S. Policy* (Santa Monica: RAND, R-4178-AF, 1992). See also Michael O'Brien (ed.), *Security Issues in the Mediterranean Basin*, Proceedings of a Conference sponsored by the National Defense University, Naples, 9–10 April 1992.

Morocco will or should remain the focus of U.S. relations in the Maghreb at a time when Algeria is experiencing dramatic change and old geostrategic imperatives such as the control of Gibraltar have faded.

The process of decolonization and the rise of the American presence in the Mediterranean during and after World War II ushered in what one North African writer has termed "the era of the American Mediterranean."[10] An important question for the future concerns the appropriate extent of American involvement in the security of the Maghreb and the western Mediterranean in the wake of the East-West competition. The United States is likely to retain a substantial residual military presence in the Mediterranean as Europe's security concerns shift southward. Indeed, it is possible to envision a future in which the United States maintains little or no forces on the European continent, with a relative concentration of naval and air presence on the European periphery. This presence would be relevant to European security but would be aimed in large measure at risks emanating from beyond the Mediterranean basin itself. At the same time, it would also serve as a hedge against the limited ability of actors along the southern littoral to interfere with shipping and military movements in times of crisis.

DEMOGRAPHIC TRENDS AND SECURITY CONSEQUENCES

The combined population of Algeria, Libya, Morocco, and Tunisia is growing at a rate of approximately 2.7 percent annually. This could result in a total population of around 142 million by 2025 (the 1992 population is roughly 64 million). The number of people under 15 years of age will increase to roughly 30 percent of the total in the same period.[11] Europe has been the major destination for economic

---

[10]See Faysal Yachir, *The Mediterranean: Between Autonomy and Dependency* (Tokyo: The United Nations University, 1989). Previous epochs were dominated by European power, or earlier still, by the competition between European (Spanish) and Muslim (Ottoman) influence in the Mediterranean. The latter struggle is exhaustively treated in Fernand Braudel, *The Mediterranean and the Mediterranean World in the Age of Philip II* (New York: Harper and Row, 1972, first published 1949).

[11]An amalgam of World Bank and U.N. estimates. See Giorgio Gomel, "Migrations Toward Western Europe: Trends, Outlook, Policies," *The International Spectator*, April-June 1992; and data from the Economist Intelligence Unit Survey of North Africa,

migrants and refugees from the Maghreb, accounting for roughly 2.5 million out of Europe's total migrant labor force of 7 million. As Europe's immigration policies tighten with the implementation of the Schengen Agreements and movement toward a single European market, new migrants will find it difficult if not impossible to enter the European labor market legally. These restrictions have been given impetus by the rise of anti-immigrant, right-wing political parties in western Europe and the growing prominence of the immigration issue on centrist political agendas.

The closing of the migration safety valve comes at a time when the Maghrebi economies are facing economic collapse and considerable uncertainty about access to traditional markets in Europe as the progress toward a single market introduces new nontariff barriers to trade (in theory, the North African countries have unrestricted access to the European market). In the future, agricultural produce from the southern Mediterranean countries will also be subject to a system of quotas that will strongly affect the economic outlook for Morocco and Tunisia.[12] Observers and politicians on both sides of the Mediterranean are concerned that demographic pressures, failing economies, and Europe's growing intolerance of Maghrebi immigrants will contribute directly to political instability along the southern shore. Should radical Islam triumph in Algeria or elsewhere in the region, southern Europe could well face an additional influx of middle-class "boat people," refugees from revolution, intolerance, and declining economic opportunity.[13]

On a broader and more emotive level, the stark disparity in demographic trends between north and south in the Mediterranean raises European fears about the long-term balance of influence in the Mediterranean, and the possibility that Maghrebi migrants in Europe will become more politically assertive, perhaps in response to future crises in the Middle East. At the same time, Maghrebi observers are beginning to consider the political and security consequences of the

---

in George Joffe, "European Security and the New Arc of Crisis," *New Dimensions in International Security*, IISS Annual Conference Papers (Adelphi Paper No. 265, London: IISS, Winter 1991–1992), pp. 62–63.

[12]Joffe, *op. cit.*, p. 63.

[13]See Gil Loescher, *Refugee Movements and International Security* (Adelphi Paper No. 268, London: IISS, 1992).

Mediterranean as "an Islamic sea."[14] The changing cultural and political character of the Mediterranean basin is of obvious concern to Europeans. It is also an issue of considerable relevance to the future of U.S. relations with Morocco, Algeria, and Tunisia, and even more broadly, the future of the U.S. presence in and around the Mediterranean. A Mediterranean environment increasingly defined by its Islamic-Western and north-south cleavages will change the climate for deterrence and security cooperation facing the United States as an extra-Mediterranean power. The evolution of the Mediterranean along these lines could create new regional flash-points and deepen the consequences of existing ones. In the Adriatic, we are already witnessing the effects of a Balkan crisis evolving *inter alia* along Muslim-Christian lines. Western policy toward Bosnia's Muslims is watched with a critical eye throughout the Arab and Islamic worlds, not least in North Africa.

EUROPE AND THE U.S. BETWEEN NORTH AND SOUTH

The key roles in the political and economic engagement of the Maghreb countries are likely to be played by Europeans, either on a national or collective basis. The mounting European interest in mitigating the consequences of instability, underdevelopment, and population pressure in the Maghreb makes this a natural development.[15] It has already found expression in the dialogue within the "Five plus Five" grouping, bringing France, Spain, Italy, Portugal, and Malta together with the countries of the Arab Maghreb Union—Mauritania, Morocco, Algeria, Tunisia, and Libya. On the economic front, the EC has been engaged in a general attempt to revive its Mediterranean

---

[14]In historical terms, the Mediterranean as a largely Islamic sea would not be a novel concept as the Ottoman dominance of the eastern basin and the southern shore of the Mediterranean from the 13th through 17th centuries demonstrates. Of course, a preponderance of Islamic believers around the Mediterranean basin does not necessarily imply a preponderance of power (see Braudel, op. cit.); and Bernard Lewis, *The Muslim Discovery of Europe* (New York: W. W. Norton, 1972). Competition in an earlier epoch is addressed in Henri Pirenne, *Mohammed and Charlemagne* (London: Unwin University Books, 1974, first published in 1939).

[15]See for example, Alvaro Vasconcelos, "The New Europe and the Western Mediterranean," *NATO Review*, No. 5. October 1991; Roberto Aliboni, "Europe Between East and South: Security and Development Cooperation," *The International Spectator*, April-June 1992.

policy.[16] Existing energy ties will expand with the implementation of new agreements for the export of Algerian natural gas to Spain and elsewhere in Europe.[17] A high-capacity pipeline across Morocco to Gibraltar is planned for this purpose. On completion, the pipeline will not only deepen the economic links between Algeria, Morocco, and Europe but may also increase political and strategic interdependence on a trilateral level. On the military front, European efforts to build an independent defense identity around the Western European Union (WEU) have been given impetus by the need to address security problems outside the NATO area, many of which are in the south (this is even more evident if one includes the Balkans in the definition of the "south"). Indeed, the WEU has begun to explore cooperation with Maghreb states in much the same manner as NATO has attempted in the East through the North Atlantic Cooperation Council.

Absent a pressing geostrategic rationale for active involvement ashore in Africa, including North Africa, it will be difficult to keep the region on the American foreign policy agenda. To the extent that the United States remains involved in the region after the Cold War, there will be significant opportunities to refashion bilateral relations free of the requirements of containment.[18] As the pronounced effect of the Gulf War on Morocco, Algeria, and Tunisia demonstrated, U.S. freedom of action in fashioning policy toward the Maghreb— including the balance between U.S. and European opportunities in the region—will turn to a great extent on developments in the Middle East as a whole.

With the end of the Cold War, it has become fashionable to refer to a looming competition along north-south lines.[19] Whether or not such

---

[16]Alan Riding, "European Nations Planning a New Focus on North Africa," *New York Times*, 31 July 1990; Claude Lorieux, "Unification et Europe: Les Defis du Maghreb," *Figaro*, 27 July 1990; and Francis Ghiles, "Maghreb States Seek to Strengthen Ties with EC," *Financial Times*, 25 July 1990.

[17]"Agreement with Spain Concluded on Natural Gas," *FBIS-NES*, 10 June 1992, p. 9.

[18]On this general point, see Michael Clough, *U.S. Policy Toward Africa and the End of the Cold War* (New York: Council on Foreign Relations, 1992).

[19]For a balanced assessment of the "southern" dimension of the new European security environment, see Edward Mortimer, *European Security After the Cold War* (Adelphi Paper No. 271, London: IISS, 1992), pp. 35–46.

a competition is inevitable in strategic terms, it is clearly a leading source of concern for foreign and security policy elites in the Third World. The concentration of demographic, migratory, and proliferation problems in the western Mediterranean—like the Rio Grande in the North American context, a place where the political and economic divide between the rich north and the poor south is most pronounced—makes the Maghreb a leading test case for the north-south confrontation thesis. Indeed, at least part of the significance of the recent Gulf War experience for publics and elites across the Maghreb derives from its potential precedent-setting character. As one observer has asserted, "The Gulf War was a spectacular example of Northern military force being deployed in the South, and it is unlikely to be the last."[20] The considerable level of support across North Africa for the Iraqi position during and after the war (national responses are examined in more detail in Chapters 3–5) flows in large part from long-standing pro-Palestinian and anti-Gulf sentiments. At a more abstract level, there has also been a strong perception that Europe and the United States are looking for ways to reorient their security policies along north-south lines. Notably, this perception of a new Cold War is not confined to anti-Western figures or opinion "in the street," but is widespread, cuts across class and political lines, and helps shape attitudes on issues as diverse as immigration policy and proliferation.

PROLIFERATION RISKS AND CONSEQUENCES

The two Gulf wars drew attention to the political and strategic consequences of nuclear, chemical, and ballistic missile proliferation for Europe and the United States.[21] This experience was also watched closely by governments and observers across North Africa. Proliferation issues were, of course, already an established part of relations with Libya; indeed, Tripoli's chemical, nuclear, and ballistic

---

[20]Edward J. Mortimer, "New Fault Lines: Is a North-South Confrontation Inevitable in Security Terms?" *New Dimensions in International Security* (IISS Annual Conference Papers, Adelphi Paper No. 296, London: IISS, Winter 1991–1992), p. 81.

[21]See Thomas L. McNaugher, "Ballistic Missiles and Chemical Weapons: The Legacy of the Iran-Iraq War," *International Security*, Fall 1990; and Ron Matthews, "Dangerous New Twist in the Middle East's Arms Race Spiral," *RUSI Journal*, Winter 1990.

missile programs have played the leading role in drawing Western attention to the country. To this may be added British concerns about Libyan links to the Irish Republican Army, and French attention to Libyan involvement in Chad. Algeria's experimental nuclear program and alleged search for ballistic missiles of up to 1000 km range became the focus of Western scrutiny. Even Mauritania found itself at the center of Spanish and Portuguese concerns with unconfirmed reports that Iraq had established ballistic missile sites in the country capable of reaching Madeira and the Canaries. Morocco and Tunisia, although not identified with efforts to acquire weapons of mass destruction, began to speculate on the effects of such programs on their own security as well as north-south relations. The Tunisian leadership faced an additional dilemma in trying to reconcile the negative effects of Libyan and Algerian weapons programs on Tunisia's security while accommodating popular (and some degree of elite) enthusiasm for redressing the strategic imbalance between the Arab world and the West, above all Israel.[22]

Looking beyond the Gulf experience, it is likely that the general search for geopolitical weight and international prestige will provide strong incentives for proliferation in North Africa. Algerians are well aware of the attention that their nascent nuclear program has drawn in the West at a time when Algeria can no longer play the political trump of nonalignment.[23] Maghrebi leaders, once leading proponents of naval arms control as a means of reducing the military weight of the superpowers in the Mediterranean, are now far more likely to speak of the right of regional powers to acquire the means of self defense and technological development unencumbered by restrictive regimes.[24] As the republics of the former Soviet Union begin to place their expertise and surplus equipment on the world market,

---

[22]On proliferation trends in North Africa generally, see Jed Snyder, "Proliferation Threats to Security in NATO's Southern Region," in O'Brien, op. cit. On the nuclear dimension, see Lewis A. Dunn, *Containing Nuclear Proliferation* (Adelphi Paper No. 263, London: IISS, Winter 1991).

[23]Algeria's nuclear and ballistic missile ambitions are addressed in more detail in Chapter 4.

[24]See Howard LaFranchi, "Algerians Defend Nuclear Program," *Christian Science Monitor*, May 3, 1991, p. 6; and Steven Emerson, "The Post-War SCUD Boom," *Wall Street Journal*, July 10, 1991.

North Africa may emerge as an attractive outlet for modern attack submarines among other conventional and unconventional technologies.[25]

What might be the effects of conventional and unconventional weapon proliferation along the southern shore of the Mediterranean on European and U.S. security? By the year 2000, it is *possible* that every southern European capital will be within range of ballistic missiles fired from Algeria or Libya (the same will hold in the eastern Mediterranean with regard to missiles based in Syria; Ankara is already just within range of Syrian Scud-Cs).[26] A Libyan move into northern Tunisia would pose an even more immediate missile threat to southern Europe. Uncertainty about whether such systems are carrying chemical or other unconventional warheads would raise the strategic significance of these weapons. The *potential* for political blackmail, however weak, would exist, especially in times of crisis. Unimpeded proliferation across the Mediterranean would reinforce the role of southern Europe as the new "front line" in direct as well as indirect terms (i.e., beyond the softer issue of migration). It could well give additional impetus to the development of an independent European defense capability if southern Europe anticipates a substantial reduction in the U.S. presence in the Mediterranean. Greater interest in ballistic missile defenses will be an obvious outgrowth of anxiety about the strategic threat from the south. This will introduce new tensions into French policy where the need to maintain the viability of France's independent nuclear forces will conflict with the desire to counter a proximate threat to French territory.

The security consequences of Mediterranean proliferation trends may be felt first and most directly in Europe. But U.S. interests and strategic freedom of action will also be affected. Leaving aside the risks that nuclear, chemical, and ballistic missile proliferation would pose for American intervention forces in regional contingencies, an environment in which southern European population centers may be held at risk could affect the calculus of transatlantic cooperation

---

[25]See Andrew Slade, "Upheaval Fails to Halt Building of Warships," *Financial Times,* May 19, 1992.

[26]See Gerald Seib, "Missile Race in Middle East Continues Despite U.S. Efforts to Stall Buildup," *Wall Street Journal,* June 8, 1992, p. 6; and Michael Wines, "Third World Seeks Advanced Arms," *New York Times,* March 26, 1991.

in future crises. Countries such as Portugal, Spain, France, and Italy will have to weigh more carefully the benefits of cooperation against the costs of becoming a target for radical regimes. The unprecedented degree of cooperation that the United States enjoyed across southern Europe during the Gulf War owed a great deal to the *de facto* sanctuarization of the region (apart from a risk of terrorist attack and the obscure ballistic missile threat referred to above). The future environment may be less secure and less amenable to close cooperation. If the U.S. air and naval presence in the Mediterranean region declines, the perceived risks of cooperation will increase, and the political incentives for offering access to facilities and airspace, not to mention the contribution of forces, will decline. It is most likely that southern European and Maghrebi allies such as Morocco will still find it in their national interest to cooperate with the United States in regional crises. But this outcome will be more predictable if the United States is seen to provide a significant measure of deterrence on a routine basis. This may be difficult to achieve in the absence of a permanent and visible presence in-region.

There is, however, a risk in allowing the proliferation question to dominate U.S. attitudes toward the Maghreb and north-south relations in the Mediterranean. Regional actors, not least Algeria, are already highly sensitive to the ability of their civil technology and weapons programs to confer a measure of strategic attention that they would otherwise lack. At the same time, the portrayal of the new European security environment in stark north-south or Western versus Islamic terms risks deepening the prevailing sense of insecurity in the Maghreb in the wake of the Cold War. Above all, Europe and the United States, as well as existing regimes in the Maghreb, share a strong interest in preventing a dangerous interaction between Islamic radicalism, north-south tensions, and opportunities for proliferation.

INTERNAL AND EXTERNAL CHALLENGES

Morocco, Algeria, and Tunisia face substantial problems of adjustment in the new strategic environment, above all in redefining their relations with the West. Despite some broad similarities, the nature of these challenges varies considerably from Rabat to Tunis.[27] However, perceptions across the region are congruent with regard to the primacy of domestic security concerns, including their role as determinants of regional behavior. The following chapters address national perspectives on the changes in the Mediterranean and international scene, the prospects for internal stability, regional security concerns, and the outlook for bilateral relations with the United States.

---

[27]An excellent recent survey of trends in the three core countries of the Maghreb can be found in Claire Spencer, *The Maghreb in the 1990s*, (Adelphi Paper No. 274, London: IISS, 1993).

Chapter Three

MOROCCO

A DIFFICULT ADJUSTMENT TO THE POST-COLD WAR WORLD

King Hassan has described Moroccans as "Arabs with a difference." One of the world's last traditional monarchies, Morocco, to an even greater extent than its Maghreb neighbors, has been shaped by its geographic isolation from the eastern Arab world (the Mashrek) and its relatively brief experience of colonial domination. Politically, Morocco has pursued Arab, Maghrebi, African, and Mediterranean vocations. In strategic terms, its importance has derived from its position at the entrance to the Mediterranean, astride one of the world's busiest waterways and the sea line of communication stretching from the Atlantic to Suez and beyond. Morocco's location, together with King Hassan's ability and willingness to play an active diplomatic and military role in Africa and the Middle East, gave the country considerable importance during the Cold War and provided the basis for strong ties to the United States and Europe.

The end of the East-West competition and the virtual disappearance of any significant naval threat to the West's sea lines of communication through Gibraltar give rise to a justified fear of strategic neglect in Rabat. In many respects, Morocco's problem of adjustment to post-Cold War realities is the most difficult of the three countries surveyed in this report. Lacking Algeria's resources and reputation for Third World leadership, lacking Tunisia's more highly developed pattern of economic and cultural ties to Europe, and having enjoyed very close security ties to the United States, the development of a new world view and rationale for strategic attention is bound to be difficult. Moroccan officials have made only the most tentative progress toward redefining the country's role, a task made more difficult by the EC's arm's length attitude toward Morocco and the lack of debate on international issues outside a small elite (the circle of opinion that is influential in the royal administration is, of course, smaller still).

In political, economic, and cultural terms, the outlook of the Moroccan elite continues to be heavily influenced by the connection with France. In regional security matters, the relationship with the United States is given higher priority. Indeed, the movement toward an independent European defense identity is greeted with some suspicion in Rabat, especially to the extent that WEU and southern European interests are increasingly focused southward. As elsewhere in the Maghreb, there is a growing fear of deterioration in north-south relations, relations between Islam and the West, and relations between the EC and North Africa, all of which would affect Morocco's opportunities for political and economic development. Europe's growing hostility to immigrants is a subject of both elite and popular concern, and the Moroccan press gives prominent treatment to accounts of anti-immigrant incidents in Europe.   There is a widespread perception in official and academic circles that with the end of the Cold War the Iron Curtain has been dismantled only to be resurrected along a north-south axis. Moreover, the xenophobic tendencies in France, Germany, and elsewhere are taken as an emerging hallmark of the new Europe and not simply as a transitory phenomenon.

INTERNAL CHALLENGES

In the eyes of Moroccan and foreign observers, the prospects for stability in Morocco have always been closely tied to the position and behavior of the monarchy. King Hassan continues to play a critical role in mitigating and channeling destabilizing social, economic, and political forces within the country. Hassan, who ascended the throne on the death of his father Mohammed V in 1961, has been extraordinarily skillful in marshaling traditional and nationalist images to reinforce his legitimacy. In this context, the king's ability to claim direct descent from the Prophet Mohammed and to emphasize his position as "Commander of the Faithful" has been essential. The failure of at least two dramatic assassination and coup attempts in 1971 and 1972 has further contributed to the king's aura of charismatic legitimacy or *baraka*.[1] On the foreign policy and security front, King Hassan has successfully used the western Sahara dispute as a nationalist rallying point, diverting attention from domestic problems that might otherwise provide fertile ground for Islamic and liberal-left opposition groups. The king's active diplomatic role as an Arab moderate and self-styled broker between the West and the Arab world has not only allowed Morocco to "punch above its weight" in international affairs but has also contributed to the internal prestige of the monarchy.[2]

Morocco faces formidable social, economic, and political challenges. The current population of over 24 million (according to a 1988 census) is growing at roughly 2.5 percent annually. Over 50 percent of the population is under 20 years of age. Official unemployment hovers around 15 percent but is probably much higher, especially in the 15–25 year age group where it may be as high as 30 percent. The difficult employment picture has driven large numbers of Moroccans (estimates range up to one million) abroad, half of whom are resident in France.[3] Their remittances have been an important source of income for Morocco and constitute approximately 7 percent of GNP. Unlike some of its Maghreb neighbors, the Moroccan economy is not in an obvious state of crisis. Inflation throughout the 1980s ran at an average of 7.7 percent, but was accompanied in the latter half of the decade by extremely unpopular wage controls. GDP growth averaged 2.3 percent from 1965–1989 but less than 1 percent over the last decade.[4]

---

[1] See Rone Tempest, "Morocco's Hassan Survives Africa's Political Minefield," *Los Angeles Times*, 16 April 1991; and Parker, *op. cit.*, pp. 21–36.

[2] A comprehensive interview with the king covering internal and external issues was published in *Liberation* (Paris), 7 July 1992. The text of the interview is reproduced in "Hassan Interviewed," *FBIS-NES*, 9 July 1992, pp. 17–20.

[3] Estimates from *North Africa: Economic Structure and Analysis* (London: Economist Intelligence Unit, 1991), pp. 133–135.

[4] See Mustafa Benyakhlef, "Morocco and Stability Issues," in O'Brien, *op. cit.*, p. 152. A general review of Morocco's economic performance is provided in George Joffe, "Morocco," *South*, September 1989.

An austerity program introduced in the mid-1980s at the behest of the International Monetary Fund and aimed at reducing Morocco's foreign debt of $22 billion has aggravated economic hardship for the majority of Moroccans. The removal of subsidies on key foodstuffs and the general perception of a deterioration in living standards contributed to riots in Casablanca in 1981 and 1984, the former leaving as many as 600 dead. More recent riots in Fez in December 1990, in which at least 33 people were killed, have also been ascribed to widespread economic frustration.[5] Twenty-eight percent of the urban population and 45 percent of the rural population are estimated to be living in poverty as defined in a recent U.N.D.P. report.[6]

The existence of large numbers of unemployed or underemployed young people, facing dismal prospects at home and increasingly little opportunity for legal work abroad, contributes to a deteriorating social landscape. At the same time, the traditional weight of the countryside in Moroccan society is decreasing as large numbers of people move to the outskirts of the larger cities in search of jobs and social services. Taken together with the rise of a small but highly visible new class of urban entrepreneurs, many of whom owe (or just as significant, are perceived to owe) their success to favoritism and corruption, the changing balance between urban and rural Morocco is having a pronounced effect on the political scene.[7] Tribal and clan ties, a traditional source of royal power, have largely been replaced by a new clientalism based on money as Moroccan society becomes more urban. The king has skillfully placed himself and his circle at the center of this new system of patronage, but some observers fear that in doing so he has eroded the legitimacy and prestige of the monarchy. As the Moroccan economy deteriorates in distributional terms—by this measure it rates very poorly even by Maghrebi standards—the monarchy itself is likely to come under increasing political pressure.[8]

---

[5]See "33 Die in 2-Day Riot in Morocco," *New York Times*, 17 December 1991.

[6]*Human Development Report, 1991* (New York: United Nations, 1991).

[7]On this issue and the pressures for reform, see "The Maghreb: A New Chance to Put Couscous on the Table," *The Economist*, 10 December 1988.

[8]The specific effects of macroeconomic stabilization measures on equity in Morocco are discussed in Christian Morrisson, *Adjustment and Equity in Morocco* (Paris: OECD, 1991).

Crown Prince Sidi Mohammed is not rated highly by foreign observers and is unlikely to prove as popular or as capable as his father.[9] Demands for social justice and freer political expression could well produce a popular explosion in the absence of King Hassan's agile exercise of power. Sidi Mohammed may inherit a legacy of tactical success but strategic failure in the lack of robust political institutions outside the monarchy.

Radical Islam has not evolved to the point of threatening the established order in Morocco. Active Islamist groups in Morocco range from the moderate and popular Al-Jamaa movement of Abdesalam Yacine, to the various militant splinter groups deriving from Adelkarim Mottai's Islamic Youth Society. The government has moved strongly against the latter group and others, sentencing activists to long prison terms and, occasionally, to death. The large number of prisoners being held under harsh conditions since the riots of 1984 and 1990 has given rise to increasing criticism of Morocco on human rights grounds in the EC and elsewhere.[10] The effectiveness of the Moroccan security apparatus in penetrating and suppressing Islamic groups, combined with the inability of disparate Islamist factions to form a united front, have thus far insured that militant Islam remains a latent political force in Morocco.[11]

The king's strong ties to mainstream Sunni Islam, and his careful attention to the traditional and religious aspects of the monarchy, are widely seen as important factors in the ability of the current Moroccan regime to prevent the emergence of a potent militant Muslim challenge. Developments in Algeria have nonetheless given

---

[9]It is worth noting, however, that King Hassan was also given poor chances for survival after his father's death. The current king reportedly told a recent interviewer that "when I ascended to the throne, people said I would not last more than six months." Tempest, "Morocco's Hassan Survives Africa's Political Minefield."

[10]Gilles Perrault, in *Notre Ami le Roi*, published in France in 1990, accused the Hassan regime of systematic human rights violations. The publicity attending its publication severely strained relations between the two countries. See Steven Greenhouse, "Book About Morocco's King Straining Ties with France," *New York Times*, 11 November 1990. Amnesty International has made similar accusations. See also Omar Bendourou, "The Exercise of Political Freedoms in Morocco," *The Review (International Commission of Jurists)*, No. 40, 1988.

[11]See Henry Munson, Jr., "Morocco's Fundamentalists," *Government and Opposition*, Summer 1991.

rise to a new wave of concern about the king's vulnerability—to democracy as well as militant Islam—as the social crisis in Morocco deepens.[12] An Islamic regime in Algiers with internationalist objectives would put Rabat under considerable pressure, and might even be in a position to provide active support to sympathetic groups within Morocco and politically active Moroccans abroad. Even in the absence of a well-organized Islamic challenge to King Hassan, the Moroccan regime is likely to take increasing account of Islamist sentiments in framing its foreign and security policy. The routine management of relations with the United States and Europe may not be strongly affected. But the behavior of the Moroccan regime on key questions, including the Arab-Israeli dispute and policy toward Iraq and Libya, could be shaped by the need to assuage religious opinion. In this context, it is notable that Islamists played an important role in the officially sanctioned anti-Western demonstrations in Rabat during the Gulf crisis. The fate of Muslims in Bosnia could emerge as a leading factor in attitudes toward the United States and Europe.

The crisis in Algeria will very likely be used by the king as an excuse to postpone real democratization in Morocco. King Hassan describes himself as a constitutional monarch, and active opposition parties have existed in Morocco for decades. Nonetheless, most observers regard the Moroccan system as at best quasi-democratic. In some areas, including foreign policy and security matters, royal control is exercised along traditional and absolute lines. Unauthorized groups cannot function effectively, and the main opposition parties, the nationalist Istiqlal and the Socialist Union of Popular Forces, stop well short of attacking the monarchy. As the widely shared desire for national unity in the face of the Western Sahara crisis fades, calls for fuller democracy, including unfettered elections, have become more insistent. To date, the King has shown little inclination to change the pattern of autocratic rule in Morocco, preferring to sidestep political reform by means of economic concessions and foreign policy initiatives. The combination of internal and external pressure for reform

---

[12]See "North Africa: Ripple Effect," *The Economist*, 4 January 1992; and Howard LaFranchi, "Morocco Inches Toward Reform," *The Christian Science Monitor*, 22 May 1991.

will make this an increasingly difficult path to follow.[13] The lack of reform and the failure to develop modern political institutions will heighten the risk of instability after King Hassan passes from the scene. It will also encourage Moroccan isolation from Europe and the United States in the absence of Cold War imperatives.

THE GULF WAR AND ITS AFTERMATH: A DIFFICULT BALANCING ACT

In the immediate aftermath of the Iraqi invasion of Kuwait, Rabat issued a statement strongly condemning Iraqi aggression. In a show of support for the Gulf monarchies and the U.N. coalition, King Hassan sent a substantial military contingent to the region: 1,200 troops to Saudi Arabia and 5,000 to the United Arab Emirates.[14] Very rapidly, however, the tide of popular sympathy for Iraq, evident across the Maghreb, began to influence the stance of the Moroccan government. Faced with mounting pressure from opposition groups and confronted with a situation that could become uncontrollable and threaten the stability of the regime, King Hassan began to distance himself from the multinational action in the Gulf, stating that "although our position on Iraq's invasion of Kuwait is opposed to theirs, our hearts are with the Iraqis."[15] The government loosened its control over strikes and demonstrations and allowed a number of anti-Western protests, including a rally of 200,000–300,000 people in Rabat. The Moroccan deployment to the Gulf was continued but with the king's insistence that it was a purely symbolic contribution.

The Gulf crisis pointed to the ability of events in the Middle East to have a rapid and pronounced effect on Moroccan opinion, an effect the Moroccan regime could ignore only at its peril. Had the United

---

[13]See "North Africa: Ripple Effect," *The Economist*, 4 January 1992, pp. 34–35; and Parker, *op. cit.*, p. 33.

[14]In conversations in Morocco in the spring of 1992, the author encountered a widespread public belief that most of these troops never returned to Morocco, with the implication that they had become casualties in the war. In fact, Moroccan troops were not engaged in battle, and a more sensible explanation is that they remained in the region at the service of the Saudi and UAE governments.

[15]Quoted in Steven Greenhouse, "War Puts Strain on North Africa," *New York Times*, 6 February 1991. See also Francis Ghiles, "Crisis in the Gulf: Saddam—A Robin Hood in North African Eyes," *Financial Times*, 22 August 1990.

States made extensive use of the facilities at Ben Guerir which Rabat had offered to Washington at the start of the crisis, the outpouring of popular discontent might well have taken on a more serious anti-American character. In the event, the use of Spanish facilities did become the focus of considerable anger in Morocco despite conciliatory visits by Spanish officials.[16]

What might be the effect of an Arab-Western clash in the Maghreb itself? King Hassan's reluctance to endorse a hard line policy toward Libya in the dispute over the 1988 Lockerbie bombing and the sabotage of a French airliner over the Sahara in 1989 is at least partly a result of his sensitivity to public and regional opinion. Given the Gulf experience, Rabat would view an American intervention in Libya with the gravest concern. The palace has taken great care to pursue a course of neutral diplomacy, counseling against the imposition of sanctions in the absence of proof of Libyan complicity in the bombings.[17] In attempting to steer a pragmatic course with regard to Libya, Rabat has had to face additional and complicating pressures arising from its position (through 1993) as a rotating member of the U.N. Security Council. Morocco is likely to abide by the U.N. consensus on policy toward Libya, but will resist going further even at U.S. insistence.

NORTH-SOUTH RELATIONS

Although Moroccan officials like to cite their country's proximity to the EC as a positive factor for economic and political development, the reality of current relations between Rabat and Brussels has been mixed. The future of Morocco's trading status with the EC is uncertain as Europe moves toward a single market. Human rights concerns emerged as a leading obstacle to relations with the EC in 1992, impeding the distribution of funds allocated for Morocco under the EC's Mediterranean assistance program. Severe restrictions on Moroccan migration, and the perceived mistreatment of Moroccan workers already resident in Europe, have combined to foster a sense of increasing distance between north and south. For many

---

[16]See Peter Bruce, "Europe's Other Front Line," *Financial Times*, 14 September 1990.

[17]Judith Miller, "Moroccan Rejects Hard Line on Libya," *New York Times*, 2 March 1992.

Moroccans, the Mediterranean is becoming more a barrier than a bridge at a time when a closer EC connection could provide a valuable context for Moroccan policy.

Together with Algeria and Tunisia, Morocco has been the beneficiary of a cooperation agreement with the EC, which allows preferential access to the European market. This agreement expired in 1992 and will be replaced by a theoretically more open system under which Moroccan goods will have to compete on an equal footing with those from Spain, Portugal, and elsewhere in Europe. Most observers believe that it will be difficult for Moroccan producers to maintain their position under these conditions.[18] The evolution of Morocco's trade relationship with the EC will be critical to the country's development prospects, as well as to north-south relations in the western Mediterranean, not least because Rabat relies on Europe for 65 percent of its current imports and 66 percent of its exports.[19] Nonetheless, the EC's desire to reinvigorate its policy toward the southern Mediterranean countries, together with the increasingly troubled situation in Algeria, is having a salutory effect on relations between Brussels and Rabat. Evidence of this can be seen in the EC's December 1992 initiative aimed at negotiating a landmark treaty of political and economic cooperation with Morocco.[20]

Regulation of the flow of Moroccan workers to and from Spain, and onward to the rest of Europe, has emerged as a more pressing issue with the progressive dismantling of internal barriers to movement within the EC. On the whole, there has been reasonable cooperation between Madrid and Rabat in this area.[21] Both governments are concerned that a deterioration of relations over the migration issue could encourage public animosity in Morocco, with potentially serious implications for the security of the Spanish enclaves of Ceuta and Melilla (see below). Over the past year, the issue of illegal migration has attracted closer attention on both sides of the straits with

---

[18]See, for example, "South Survey: Morocco (Life on the Edge of the Community)," *South*, September 1989, p. 87.

[19]1991 estimates provided by U.S. Embassy, Rabat. Europe is also the overwhelming source of foreign direct investment, with France providing the largest share.

[20]*The Economist*, January 9, 1993, p. 38.

[21]See "Migration Agreement with Morocco Signed," *FBIS-WEU*, 18 February 1992, p. 32.

frequent and well publicized incidents of small craft sinking off Gibraltar and Algeciras.[22]

REGIONAL SECURITY CONCERNS

Morocco's external security concerns are overwhelmingly of a south-south nature. Nonetheless, two security issues are of direct relevance to north-south relations as seen from Rabat. The first is the general movement toward a European defense identity and, possibly, the development of an independent European capacity for intervention outside the NATO area. Moroccan observers view this trend in serious terms, especially in the context of the southern European perception of a "threat from the south." Despite the fact that Spain has been a leading supplier of military equipment to Morocco, the growing Spanish role in NATO and the Western European Union is interpreted as evidence of Madrid's desire for reinsurance against risks emanating from North Africa.[23]

Ceuta and Melilla

Second, Rabat is keenly aware of the role that the defense of the Spanish enclaves of Ceuta and Melilla plays in Spanish planning.[24] The two enclaves have been in Spanish hands since the late 15th century (before this they had been Portuguese) and are treated as integral parts of the national territory under Spain's 1978 constitution. Ceuta and Melilla are small (eight and four and a half square miles, respectively) and difficult to defend without seizing a substantial defensive perimeter on Moroccan territory sufficient to place the enclaves out of artillery range. To date, King Hassan has been careful to avoid the suggestion of a military solution to the problem of the enclaves, and has even hesitated to press the issue of Moroccan sovereignty within the U.N. or the Arab League. In any case, policy-

---

[22]See "The Short Cut," *The Economist*, 12 September 1992, p. 56.

[23]Spain continues to conduct annual joint military exercises with Morocco. A bilateral Treaty of Friendship and Cooperation has been concluded, but has yet to be ratified by either country. The agreement is silent on the thorny question of the Spanish enclaves in Morocco.

[24]The role of the enclaves in Spanish planning is addressed in Lesser, *op. cit.*

makers in Rabat and Madrid are well aware of the changing demographic balance within the enclaves and the increasingly Moroccan character of the towns as the Spanish population declines and the Moroccan population grows. Moderate Moroccans are confident that demographic change and the eventual return of Gibraltar to Spain make the return of the enclaves to Morocco a virtual certainty for the future. In more assertive nationalist and Islamist circles, there is interest in threatening violence over the territories to encourage a faster settlement.[25]

The Spanish government continues to insist that the territories are not a matter for discussion and will be defended by force if necessary. Nonetheless, it remains an open question whether any Spanish government, not least the current Socialist one, would resort to force to assert Spanish sovereignty over the enclaves in the event that large numbers of Moroccans simply entered Ceuta and Melilla and refused to leave.[26] On a routine basis, Spanish subsidies to the enclaves impose costs that may come under increasing scrutiny as the Spanish economy begins to display signs of recession following the European currency crisis of 1992. King Hassan is undoubtedly well aware of the immense dilemmas a repeat of the "Green March" into the western Sahara would pose for Madrid. Thus far, the assertion of Moroccan sovereignty over the western Sahara has provided the leading outlet for King Hassan's skillful strategy of "controlled nationalism." With an end to the Sahara issue on the horizon, the question of the enclaves may now assume a more prominent place in Moroccan rhetoric and north-south relations across the Mediterranean.

An end to the conflict in the western Sahara would release substantial forces from duty in the south and raise questions about how the Moroccan military might continue to be usefully engaged in external rather than internal matters. The redeployment of forces to the north would inevitably provoke concern in defense circles in Spain. The Spanish military garrison in the enclaves numbers approxi-

---

[25]See Aaron Segal, "Spain and the Middle East: A 15-Year Assessment," *Middle East Journal,* Vol. 45, No. 2, Spring 1991.

[26]Antonio Marquina Barrio, "Spain and Its North African Enclaves," in Joyce Lasky Shub and Raymond Carr (eds.), *Spain: Studies in Political Security* (New York: Praeger, 1985), p. 117; see also Antonio Marquina Barrio, "Libya, the Maghreb and Mediterranean Security," in *Prospects for Security in the Mediterranean, Part III.*

mately 20,000 (the garrisons were substantially reinforced during the Gulf crisis). A military crisis over the enclaves would pose the risk of rapid escalation, since an effective Spanish response would, as mentioned above, involve the seizure of territory in the hinterland. More seriously, Morocco must anticipate the potential for horizontal escalation, with Spanish air and naval forces holding at risk urban, military, and industrial centers elsewhere in the Kingdom.

A clash between Spain and Morocco over the enclaves would pose substantial political and security problems for the United States. In political terms, the United States would find itself in the difficult position of having to decide whether or not to intervene on the side of a NATO ally outside the scope of Alliance treaty obligations (the Western European Union would face a more pressing situation as the defense of Ceuta and Melilla falls within the area of responsibility of the European defense arrangement). The effect of a U.S. intervention on Arab opinion must also be considered—a potentially critical consideration if sensitive Middle East negotiations are also at stake. Even if the United States stands aloof from the crisis, a confrontation across the Straits of Gibraltar would pose a serious risk to shipping in one of the world's busiest shipping lanes. Traffic through the western Mediterranean could be halted, interrupting important energy flows and imposing significant economic costs. The presence of the Sixth Fleet in the region, and the importance of being able to shift naval forces from the Mediterranean to the Atlantic, would make the crisis even more difficult to ignore. Moreover, any attack on NATO member-country aircraft or ships in the Mediterranean would bring into play treaty obligations even if fighting in and around the enclaves remained "out-of-area." If the crisis were to occur against the background of broader north-south tensions or a new conflict in the Middle East, the ability of Libya and Algeria to threaten population centers in southern Europe with air and ballistic missile attack would further complicate the U.S. position.

The Western Sahara and Relations with Algeria

The Moroccan struggle to assert its sovereignty over the western Sahara has been an integral part of King Hassan's strategy of controlled nationalism. It has also been closely tied to Moroccan security concerns with regard to its leading regional competitor, Algeria.

With the waning of the conflict between Morocco and the Polisario Front and the looming resolution of the territorial issue on Moroccan terms, the nature of Moroccan-Algerian competition is changing, with potentially important implications for regional stability.

Following the "Green March" of 1975, in which 370,000 Moroccans participated in a government-organized peaceful occupation of the Spanish Sahara, and the subsequent Spanish withdrawal, Morocco and Mauritania agreed to a division of the region and its highly touted phosphate resources (Mauritania renounced its claim to the region in 1978).[27] In response, the Polisario Front mounted an active insurgency aimed at the establishment of an independent Sahrawi state.[28] With the active backing of Algeria, and the supply of arms and materiel from the Soviet Union and Libya, the movement scored some notable early successes against the Moroccan armed forces. In recent years, the Moroccan forces have managed to contain and ultimately roll back the Polisario in the western Sahara. The construction of a massive 900-mile sand wall or berm, augmented with electronic surveillance, played an important role in preventing Polisario infiltration into Moroccan-held areas. Moroccan administrative control now extends over virtually the entire 102,000 square mile territory, including all of the towns and phosphate facilities along the Atlantic coast.[29] A U.N. referendum on the political fate of the western Sahara has encountered overwhelming problems in the effort to determine who may and may not vote on the question of whether the territory is to be incorporated into

---

[27]The history of this period is explored in detail in Phillip C. Naylor, "Spain, France and the Decolonization of the Western Sahara: Parity and Paradox, 1975–1987," *Africa Today*, 3rd Quarter, 1987; and David Seddon, "Morocco and the Western Sahara," *Review of African Political Economy*, April 1987. The economic benefits of the Saharan phosphate resources have been modest, largely as a result of high transport costs and depressed prices. Fishing and other private initiatives in the region have been more successful; see Benyakhlef, *op. cit.*, p. 161.

[28]The Polisario Front is a shorter name for the "Popular Front for the Liberation of Saquia El Hamra and Rio de Oro," a reference to the territories known collectively as the western Sahara.

[29]Some observers have seen the war in the Sahara as evidence of Morocco's wider territorial and political ambitions in the region and have raised questions about the wisdom of U.S. support for King Hassan's campaign against the Polisario. See, for example, Stephen Zunes, "The United States and Morocco: The Sahara War and Regional Interests," *Arab Studies Quarterly*, Vol. 9, No. 4, Fall 1987.

Morocco or become independent.[30]   In the interim, the growing number of Moroccans induced to occupy new housing in the territory and the prospect that Moroccan parliamentary elections will include the western Sahara suggests that the political fate of the region has largely been decided outside the U.N. framework. In the unlikely case that a U.N. referendum is indeed held, the result is likely to provide *de jure* confirmation of *de facto* Moroccan control.[31] Polisario's threat to resume hostilities in the event that Rabat circumvents the U.N. referendum on self-determination is unlikely to pose a serious obstacle to the consolidation of Moroccan control.[32]

The decline of the Polisario as an effective political and military force can be traced in large part to the steady decline of Libyan and Algerian support. The political and economic crisis in Algeria has effectively brought to an end a long history of support for the Polisario and the "Democratic Arab Saharan Republic," in which Algiers acted as a conduit for Soviet military assistance. In fact, Algerian support has been in sharp decline since the reestablishment of diplomatic relations between Algeria and Morocco in 1988. Nineteen ninety-two has seen a large number of leading members of the Polisario defect to Morocco under terms negotiated by King Hassan.[33]

The prospect of an end to the conflict in the western Sahara raises a number of important issues for regional security, including the future disposition of up to 150,000 Moroccan troops and a potentially restless officer corps, the prospects for Moroccan nationalism in the

---

[30]See Kenneth Noble, "New Dispute Roils Western Sahara: Who'll Vote?" *New York Times*, 28 February 1992; "Polisario, UN End 'Helpful' Talks," Paris, *AFP*, 12 June 1992, in *FBIS-NES*, 18 June 1992, p. 20; and Paul Lewis, "UN to Ask Morocco and Sahara to Meet on Extending Cease-Fire," *New York Times*, 29 June 1990.

[31]This is not what the more optimistic observers of the U.N. initiative had in mind. The "lessons" of the Saharan experience for conflict management are explored, *inter alia*, in Bruce Maddy-Weitzman, "Conflict and Conflict Management in the Western Sahara: Is the Endgame Near?" *Middle East Journal*, Vol. 45, No. 4, Autumn 1991; and Oyvind Osterud, "War Termination in the Western Sahara," *Bulletin of Peace Proposals*, Vol. 20, No. 3, pp. 309–317, 1989.

[32]See "Polisario Threatens Resumption of War," Paris, Radio France International, 21 June 1992, in *FBIS-NES*, 24 June 1992, p. 24.

[33]Youssef Ibrahim, "West Sahara Rebel Drive Limps to a Halt," *New York Times*, 16 August, 1992.

absence of challenges south of the Atlas Mountains, and the character of the next phase in Algerian-Moroccan relations.

The conduct of the war against the Polisario required the concentration of Morocco's air and ground forces in the south of the country. This was a military necessity but also served the politically convenient purpose of removing the armed forces from key administrative centers in the north of the country and providing a legitimate external role for the military. Given the near success of two coup attempts organized by officers against King Hassan, this factor needs to be given considerable weight. An important question for the future concerns the role of the military after the Saharan war. One option would be the redeployment of some substantial part of the armed forces to the Rif in the north of the country to reinforce Rabat's control over a violent region, the center of Moroccan drug trafficking where the government's authority is tenuous. For reasons too numerous and complex to describe here, this is most unlikely.

More probable would be a general reorientation of the military forces toward the traditional threat from Algeria. Moroccans view the overt intervention of the military in Algerian politics as a dismal development, particularly in light of the assassination of President Boudiaf under circumstances that strongly suggest the involvement of the Algerian military authorities.[34] Moroccan and Algerian forces have clashed directly over territorial issues in the past, most notably during the 1963 "War of the Sands." An Islamic or strongly nationalist regime in Algiers could reassert traditional claims on Moroccan territory and renew the struggle for influence over the western Sahara with greater force. Should Moroccan fundamentalists begin to operate from Algeria, the possibility of dangerous hot-pursuit incidents cannot be excluded. This scenario, a leading concern in Tunis as well as Rabat, would be an ironic reversal of the Algerian revolutionary experience in which insurgents operated against the French from bases in Morocco.[35]

---

[34]Mohamed Boudiaf spent a long period of exile in Morocco and was regarded in some circles as well disposed toward Rabat.

[35]The pattern of infiltration and the French experience in countering it is described in Alistair Horne, *A Savage War of Peace* (New York: Viking Press, 1977).

Evidence that Algeria is exploring the option of developing a nuclear weapons capability, and has already established a nuclear program of questionable civilian utility, has not yet drawn explicit criticism from Rabat. The issue of ballistic missile proliferation has attracted more attention in Moroccan military circles. Why has Morocco been reluctant to express public concern over the Algerian proliferation risk? A plausible explanation is the relationship between the Algerian nuclear program and broader Arab aspirations. King Hassan may well find it useful to remain aloof from a debate that is increasingly framed in north-south terms. To the extent that the Algerian program can be painted in Maghrebi or Arab terms, some additional leverage might even be gained in the dialogue with Europe. Finally, in the absence of Cold War considerations, Western attention to Algerian behavior is not without utility in building a rationale for continued American and European involvement in Morocco's security.[36]

REGIONAL INTEGRATION

Rabat has assumed a leading role in the AMU, established in 1989. The grouping brings together the three core countries of Morocco, Algeria, and Tunisia along with Libya and Mauritania in an ambitious program of economic integration and political cooperation. Western analysts generally view the prospects for successful economic integration—the creation of a Maghrebi common market—as dim.[37] But the rationale for the AMU is not entirely or even primarily economic. From Rabat's perspective, the advantages of the AMU framework are largely political and strategic.[38]

---

[36]Morocco is also exploring the development of a civil nuclear power program; see "First Nuclear Plant May Be Built by 2010," MAP (Rabat), in *FBIS-NES*, 11 August 1992, p. 16.

[37]On the whole, the Maghrebi economies are more competitive than complementary, and all rely heavily on external sources for non-Mediterranean foodstuffs. See, for example, Franco Zallio, "Regional Integration and Economic Prospects of the Developing Countries to the South of the Mediterranean," *The International Spectator*, April-June 1992, pp. 55–59.

[38]See Lillian Craig Harris, "North African Unity: Fact or Fantasy?" *Arab Affairs*, Autumn 1990; Robert Mortimer, "The Maghreb at the Millennium: Prospects for the Decade," *Middle East Insight*, No. 5, 1991; Paul Balta, "Oranges, Olives, Oil—the Maghreb in Transition," *NATO's Sixteen Nations*, April 1990.

The turmoil in Algeria and the international isolation of Libya have, at least for the moment, left the AMU in a state of paralysis. Nonetheless, Morocco sees considerable advantage in the concept of regional integration—whether real or rhetorical—in the context of north-south and south-south relations. Europe's progress toward political and economic union, hardly subject to question before the events of 1992, suggested that the countries of the Maghreb would need to go beyond merely bilateral relations with the EC. The AMU might provide a forum for the conduct of north-south negotiations on a more balanced basis. Second, and in a more general sense, the AMU is one expression of the search for regional and international weight in the post-Cold War world. For Morocco in particular, it is both an additional forum for King Hassan's diplomatic activism and a useful institutional counterpart to the European grouping of Portugal, Spain, France, Italy, and Malta in the "Five plus Five" approach to western Mediterranean cooperation. Not surprisingly, all three core members regard themselves as the natural leader of Maghrebi integration and tend to cite obstructionist policies elsewhere as the leading obstacles to the AMU's success.[39] In a narrower sense, Rabat has had a strong strategic interest in a rapprochement with Algeria within the framework of the AMU as a means of undercutting the position of the Polisario in the western Sahara conflict.[40] As this conflict draws to a close on Moroccan terms, and with Algerian attention directed inward, an important incentive for regional coordination may evaporate.

PROSPECTS FOR BILATERAL RELATIONS WITH THE UNITED STATES

Moroccan officials are anxious to assert the continued strategic importance of Morocco after the Cold War and by extension the con-

---

[39]AMU may be viewed as an expression of the integrative model or cycle in the foreign relations of North Africa, an alternative to pluralism or hegemony. See I. William Zartman, "Foreign Relations of North Africa," *Annals of the American Academy* January 1987; and John Damis, "Prospects for Unity/Disunity in North Africa," *American-Arab Affairs*, No. 6, Fall 1983.

[40]Scott W. Ellison, *World Outlook*, Summer 1989; and Mary-Jane Deeb, "Inter-Maghrebi Relations since 1969: A Study of the Modalities of Unions and Mergers," *Middle East Journal*, Winter 1989.

tinuing rationale for a close bilateral relationship. In this context, it is asserted that Rabat "made all the right decisions" during the Cold War and deserves continued support. These key decisions are understood to include the establishment of a multiparty system, however imperfect; the pursuit of a market economy; an emphasis on the agricultural sector over the development of heavy industry, unfashionable in the 1960s and 1970s; and, above all, adherence to the Western camp in international affairs.

There is a palpable sense of disappointment in Rabat in the "lack of U.S. vision" in engaging Morocco and the prospective failure of Morocco's pro-Western stance in the Cold War to pay political and economic dividends. The Moroccan argument for a high degree of bilateral cooperation turns on the argument that (1) the United States owes Rabat a debt of gratitude for services in the cause of containment, and (2) the failure to preserve a close economic and political relationship will increase the risk of turmoil in Morocco and the Maghreb as a whole. As Morocco faces what is widely seen as a long-term problem of xenophobia and anti-Maghrebi sentiment in Europe, the issue of how to reorient the rationale for close relations with Washington becomes essential. The evaporation of the country's traditional strategic importance by virtue of its location at a critical maritime choke point (the prospect of a Ukrainian flotilla threatening a campaign of interdiction at the Atlantic approaches to the Mediterranean is clearly remote) poses problems of adjustment that the Moroccan elite is only beginning to explore.

Nonetheless, Morocco can still point to its role as a moderate Arab interlocutor and its potentially important role as a counterbalance to Algerian influence in North Africa as valid reasons for continuing American interest and involvement in the country. Rabat, for its part, will seek a close bilateral relationship as a means of hedging against the deterioration of relations with the EC and the threat of Algerian hegemony. King Hassan has pressed for more extensive defense cooperation with the United States, but most Moroccan observers are aware that the prospects for expanded cooperation are constrained by budgetary pressure in the United States. Less frequently cited, but equally important from the U.S. perspective, are concerns about the long-term stability of the Moroccan regime and the effect of closer security ties on the political situation in Morocco. King Hassan offered the use of Moroccan bases to support U.S. operations during the Gulf War. In the event, these facilities were hardly used. But extensive use of Moroccan bases might well have provoked a strong anti-American reaction given the widespread public support for Iraq.

U.S. security assistance is seen as a critical contribution to the maintenance of the military balance with Algeria. In this context, the most important recent development has been the provision of 20 multirole F-16s, to be delivered to Morocco from U.S. inventory in 1994 at a cost of $250 million. The aircraft, purchased with the assistance of Saudi Arabia, will operate from an improved base at Ben Guerir (with an interim base at Meknes). The purchase represents a significant shift from previous patterns of aircraft acquisition from France. The Moroccan military also receives some training and technical assistance from Germany and has explored the possibility of acquiring surplus equipment from ex-East German stocks. The growing attention to the human rights behavior of the recipients of German security assistance (e.g., Turkey) suggests that Rabat will face substantial obstacles in this area. Indeed, in the absence of Cold War imperatives, it is likely that human rights considerations will also play a larger role in U.S. deliberations on security assistance to Morocco.

Although access to Moroccan facilities and airspace could be of use to the United States in relation to future contingencies in the Middle East or the Persian Gulf, equally useful alternatives will exist in southern Europe.[41] The risk of internal and regional turmoil in the Maghreb suggests that planning for the extensive use of Moroccan bases in a crisis would represent an unwarranted exposure to the vagaries of Moroccan policy which must, in any case, tread a fine line between Arab and Western opinion. A substantial U.S. military involvement in Morocco might well have an undesirable effect on the delicately balanced political situation within the country. This risk would only grow as the question of a post-Hassan regime looms on the horizon.

Finally, the most pressing issues for Morocco in its regional and north-south relations are economic and political rather than

---

[41]The United States continues to use facilities in the south of Morocco as an emergency landing site for Space Shuttle missions.

military.   In this context, the EC and particularly the European countries of the western Mediterranean will logically play a leading role given their overwhelming position in Morocco's trade, investment, and cultural relations. Although additional American investment in Morocco would be beneficial, the prospects for a substantial influx of new capital (not to mention economic aid) cannot be good at a time when massive needs in Eastern Europe and the former Soviet Union remain unsatisfied.   If the United States continues to have interests and to remain engaged in the Maghreb, this involvement is likely to be spread more broadly across the region. An overwhelming focus on Morocco will be difficult to justify in the new strategic environment.

Chapter Four

ALGERIA

DOMESTIC TURMOIL AND THE SEARCH FOR A NEW INTERNATIONAL ROLE

The security environment as seen from Algiers is now driven almost entirely by the Islamic challenge to the political order and the deepening problem of internal stability. As a result, Algeria's potential in regional and international terms is, for the moment, dormant. A country with enormous resources and a well-established reputation for political assertiveness and international activism, Algeria has turned inward in a struggle to resolve basic questions of social and political organization.

Like its Maghrebi neighbors, Algeria faces the difficult external challenge of adjusting to a post-Cold War environment in which one superpower can no longer be played off against the other. Algeria's strategic importance can no longer be taken for granted. The Non-Aligned Movement, of which Algeria was a founding member and in which it played a leading intellectual and political role, has lost much of its significance as a framework for Algerian foreign policy.[1] Yet, looking beyond the current turmoil and regardless of its future ideological orientation, Algeria is likely to seek a new and substantial role in the Mediterranean. In this effort, Algiers can draw upon two sources of strategic weight. The first is an intangible sense of purpose and moral superiority in international affairs, traceable in large

---

[1]See Assassi Lassassi, *Non-Alignment and Algerian Foreign Policy* (Aldershot: Avebury, 1988).

39

measure to the bitter and formative experience of the revolution against French rule—a revolution that Algerians hold on a par with those of Russia and China.[2] Indeed, the frequent observation that Algerians have never really come to terms with the experience of the revolution is relevant to the country's internal as well as external dilemmas. The one thing that most Algerians will agree on is that 40 years of FLN (National Liberation Front) rule have gone very badly wrong.

The second and more tangible source of post-Cold War strategic weight is likely to be Algeria's pursuit of nuclear and ballistic missile programs. Disturbing from the point of view of European security, and with significant implications for U.S. policy and strategy, there can be little doubt that Algeria's proliferation potential will push Algeria closer to the front rank in terms of international attention and prestige within the Arab world. Of the three countries surveyed in this draft, Algeria is most clearly the state that U.S. policymakers and strategists will need to take seriously after the Cold War.

DEEPENING UNREST AND THE CHALLENGE OF RADICAL ISLAM

After years of ossified FLN rule along Arab socialist lines, the Ben Jedid government began in the late 1980s to open up the Algerian political and economic system and encourage movement toward greater pluralism and democracy. The result was a series of remarkably free elections in which the Islamic Salvation Front (FIS) scored dramatic successes at the municipal and national level.[3] In the first round of national elections in December 1991, the FIS received 3.2 million votes, or 40 percent of the votes cast. Roughly 59 percent of the electorate voted, over half for the FIS, giving the Islamists the

---

[2]Parker, *op. cit.*, p. 37. On Algeria's political development generally, see John Ruedy, *Modern Algeria: The Origins and Development of a Nation* (Bloomington: Indiana University Press, 1992).

[3]In local elections in the summer of 1990, the FIS gathered roughly 70 percent of the popular vote, gaining control of 32 of 48 provinces. On the local elections, see Fouad Ajami, "The Battle of Algiers," *The New Republic*, July 9 and 16, 1990.

support of about 25 percent of registered voters.[4] Following this stunning victory, the electoral process was interrupted by a military-led coup which removed the prime minister, prevented the second round of elections, and barred the FIS from political activity.

Should the democratic process in Algeria be resumed and new elections held, most observers believe that the FIS (or its legal equivalent) would receive as many votes or more than in the elections of December 1991. For the moment, and in the wake of a succession of leadership changes in the ruling Supreme State Council including the assassination of President Boudiaf on June 29 under circumstances pointing to the complicity of the armed forces, the democratic opening in Algeria has been derailed.[5] The government is now headed by Ali Kafi, president of the Supreme State Council, together with Belaid Abdessalam, the newly appointed prime minister. Defense Minister General Khaled Nezzar remains the unofficial power behind the post-coup government.

The interruption of the electoral process prevented the formation of an Islamic-led government. This was accomplished at the cost of driving the FIS underground, strengthening the hand of more radical factions within the Islamist movement, and encouraging the emergence of an active urban insurgency. In reality, the FIS was never a monolithic movement but rather a collection of moderate and radical groups. Prominent among the latter have been "Sin and Expiation," the "Armed Islamic Movement," and the "Army of the Prophet Mohammed." Since the coup of December 1991, and with increasing force since the imprisonment of key FIS officials (Abassi Madani and Ali Belhadj), the Algerian regime has conducted a sweeping crackdown in an effort to "roll up" the Islamist organiza-

---

[4]On the meaning of the Islamic electoral success, see Belkacem Iratni and Mohand Salah Tahi, "The Aftermath of Algeria's First Free Local Elections," *Government and Opposition (Studies on North Africa, II)*, Autumn 1991; Jacques Girardon, "A Veiled Future for Algeria," *World Press Review*, August 1990; Khalid Duran, "The Second Battle of Algiers," *Orbis*, Summer 1989; Penny Gibbins, "Algeria's Trial of Strength," *The Middle East*, July 1991; and Robert Mortimer, "Islam and Multiparty Politics in Algeria," *Middle East Journal*, Vol. 45, No. 4, Autumn 1991.

[5]"Murder in Annaba," *The Economist*, July 4, 1992; Youssef Ibrahim, "Persistent Violence and Spreading Poverty Tighten Grip on Algeria," *New York Times*, July 29, 1992.

tions.[6] The success of this effort is far from clear. Over 200 members of the security forces have been killed by Islamic extremists since the declaration of a state of national emergency in February 1992; the number of Islamic activists killed is probably larger. Perhaps as many as 600 people have died as a result of political violence since 1991. Individual terrorist attacks on the Algiers airport and elsewhere have claimed dozens of civilian lives.[7] At least 4,000 FIS supporters continue to be held under harsh conditions in five detention camps in the southern Sahara (the government has been releasing many detainees in recent months, apparently having judged that the detentions are counterproductive). Large amounts of weapons and ammunition have been stolen from military depots and police stations. It is most unlikely that the armed forces are free of Islamist sympathizers and FIS cells.

With the leading institutions in Algeria, the FLN, and the military, in public disrepute, and with substantial grass roots support for the Islamist movement, the current political situation is probably untenable. In narrower terms, the ability of the security forces to control the internal situation in the country is highly uncertain. Continued deterioration of the security situation and the outbreak of a full-blown civil war cannot be ruled out, with serious implications for stability in Tunisia and Morocco.[8] Nor is the militant Islamic challenge the only source of domestic instability. The government faces an increasing pattern of unrest among Tuareg tribesman in the far south of the country.[9]

The engine of unrest in Algeria is, as elsewhere in the Maghreb, the problem of rapid population growth coupled with economic stagnation. The effect is particularly pronounced among the legions of

---

[6]"Vows War on Islamic Fundamentalists," report of an interview with Defense Minister Khaled Nezzar in *El Moudjahid* (Algiers), *FBIS-NES*, June 29, 1992, p. 6.

[7]"Blast at Algiers Airport Kills Nine and Wounds 100," *New York Times*, August 27, 1992; "Algerians Kill Two Foes in Raid on Militants," *New York Times*, October 17, 1992. Algerians who had served—or claim to have served—in the Afghan resistance movement, the so-called *Afghani*, are alleged to be at the forefront of armed attacks on the security forces.

[8]See Youssef Ibrahim, "Crackdown Seems to Lead Algeria into Chaos," *New York Times*, August 20, 1992.

[9]"Tuaregs Discount Secession, Note Lack of Security," *FBIS-NES*, August 11, 1992, p. 8.

half-educated, unemployed young people. Unemployment in Algeria may be as high as 30 percent, even higher among those under 30 (70 percent of the Algerian population is under 30 years of age). Some 200,000 French-style baccalaureate degrees are given each year. Most of the recipients are unable to find full-time employment. At the same time, Algerians have tended to couch their economic expectations in European rather than Third World terms, a tendency encouraged by ready access to European television and radio. The inevitable frustration with an economy mired in bureaucracy and corruption—despite Algeria's substantial energy resources—strengthens the appeal of the FIS.

The post-coup regime is pinning its hopes for normalization on the destruction of the FIS as a political organization and the pursuit of economic improvement as a means of undercutting the principal source of public dissatisfaction. (An alternative theory holds that the FIS ought to be allowed back into the political process and be allowed to demonstrate its inability to solve the economic problems of the country.) Suggestions of reform and liberalization have most recently given way to calls for greater austerity and the revitalization of the state-run economy. In the view of many Algerians and foreign observers, the resurrection of the discredited economic policies of the FLN is unlikely to prove a viable approach, economically or politically. Above all, the failure to actively encourage foreign investment and internal liberalization is a reflection of the enduring autarkic outlook of the Algerian political elite.[10] Austerity is as likely to exacerbate as ameliorate the sense of political frustration. The militant Islamic groups pose an immediate political challenge. Given the scale of the demographic and economic crises in Algeria, even the most well-managed strategy of economic reform is unlikely to show results for years.

The FIS leadership, in Algeria and in exile in France, has said very little about the foreign and security policy orientation of an Islamic Algeria. Moderate FIS spokesmen have emphasized the movement's domestic agenda and the priority of moral rectification, religious in-

---

[10]The departure of Sid Ahmed Ghozali and the arrival of Belaid Abdessalam signaled a move away from economic liberalization. See Ibrahim, "Persistent Fundamentalist Violence," *op. cit.*

tegrity, and cultural revival over foreign policy goals.[11] But what little was said during the elections may be unrepresentative of views in the aftermath of the coup. The transformation of the FIS into an underground movement has strengthened the hand of more radical elements. The equivocal stance of Western and neighboring Maghrebi governments toward the elections and the subsequent coup may well have hardened attitudes even in more moderate circles. Should an Islamic regime eventually triumph in Algiers, there is a risk—although not a certainty—that it will adopt an internationalist stance, seeking to export the fundamentalist model elsewhere in the region. This has been the pattern with the Iranian-supported Islamic regime in the Sudan. An Islamic Algeria would be in a far stronger position to influence the political future of the Maghreb. The longer the delay in restoring a viable political order in Algeria—virtually inconceivable without according moderate Islamists a legitimate role—the greater the risk of a violent transition to Islamic rule with serious implications for regional stability.[12]

RESPONSE TO THE GULF WAR

The response of the Algerian government and the FIS leadership to the Gulf War provides some insight into the pressures that will continue to shape policy in Algiers regardless of the character of the regime. In the early stages of the Gulf crisis, Algiers joined its Maghrebi neighbors in condemning the Iraqi invasion of Kuwait but also proceeded to criticize the U.S. military involvement and the economic sanctions being applied against Baghdad. As the crisis deepened, and as public sentiment in Algeria echoed the pro-Iraqi manifestations elsewhere in the region, the FLN government, the FIS leadership, and other political factions (including Ahmed Ben Bella's Mouvement pour la Democratie en Algerie) began to compete with one another in an effort to embrace anti-Western public opinion. Overall, the FIS benefited from the wave of pro-Saddam demonstra-

---

[11]Youssef Ibrahim, "Islamic Plan for Algeria Is On Display," *New York Times*, January 7, 1992.

[12]See John P. Entelis, "U.S.-Maghreb Relations in a Democratic Age: The Priority of Algeria," *Middle East Insight*, January/February 1992. On Algeria as a test case for relations between Islam and the West, see Robin Wright, "Islam and Democracy," *Foreign Affairs*, Summer 1992.

tions and sentiment in Algiers, placing the Benjedid government in an even more difficult position.[13] Faced with mounting public pressure and the fear that war in the Gulf could spark a wave of revolts across North Africa, President Benjedid embarked on an active but ultimately futile round of negotiations aimed at brokering a peaceful settlement. The Algerian initiative enjoyed the backing of France and Italy and followed in the traditional Algerian role as a respected interlocutor in Middle East disputes.

In the wake of the war in the Gulf, Algerian opinion remains equivocal. The Iraqi regime is unpopular in official and elite circles. But public opinion remains supportive of Saddam Hussein. Both public and elite opinion tends to regard the outcome of the liberation of Kuwait as at best a mixed victory for the Gulf monarchies and the West. On the whole, the fact that Saddam Hussein remains in power in Baghdad is viewed with considerable admiration by most Algerians. The Gulf experience continues to be seen as a Western war against the Arab world as a whole. Even sophisticated observers express concern that such conflicts, pitting north against south and the Arab world against the West, may be typical of the post-Cold War environment. Indeed, to the extent that the nonaligned movement can be salvaged after the Cold War, Algerian officials hope that it can be recast to give the south greater diplomatic weight in its dealings with the developed world.

NORTH-SOUTH RELATIONS

Algerian perceptions of Europe have been strongly influenced by the experience of the revolution against French rule and the enduring mixture of resentment and admiration toward Paris. Members of the Algerian political elite may profess strongly anti-French views, but their patterns of analysis still follow in the French intellectual tradition. This is particularly evident in discussions of international affairs, where French attitudes and political terminology are close to the surface (e.g., the notion of the Mediterranean for the Mediterraneans). With over one million workers and their dependents resident in Europe, mostly in France, many Algerians continue

---

[13]The FIS had been the recipient of considerable Saudi financial support. Francis Ghiles, "A Fragile Fabric Comes Under Strain," *Financial Times*, January 23, 1991.

to have ties with the former metropole. This presence has caused Algerians to follow the rise of the anti-immigrant right wing in France and elsewhere with great concern. As in Morocco and Tunisia, there is a growing sense that the Mediterranean is emerging as a more formidable cultural, political, and economic barrier between north and south. With a population of some 27 million growing at roughly 3 percent per year, the progressive tightening of EC restrictions on legal migration is a cause for concern at both the government and popular level.

Beyond the issue of economic migration, legal and illegal, looms the potential for an exodus of middle-class and professional Algerians in the event that an Islamic regime takes power in Algiers. The prospect of Islamic rule is anathema to most westernized Algerians. Large numbers of skilled workers and their families would probably choose to leave an Islamic Algeria. For reasons of language and cultural familiarity as well as proximity, France would bear the brunt of this refugee movement. The result would be a serious border control and interdiction problem for the French government, and by extension, others in southern Europe. The refugee flow and the government's response would very likely have a profound effect on domestic politics in France. The existing Algerian population in France could find itself under considerable pressure and would face the threat of violence, both within its own ranks and between Algerians and French extremists.

The development of an independent European defense identity outside the NATO framework is viewed with some alarm in Algiers. This concern is reinforced by European reference to a "threat from the south," in which Algerian observers see a clear reference to their own country and its Maghrebi neighbors. As a result, Algerians who readily criticized the U.S. presence in the Mediterranean during the Cold War are now giving some thought to the importance of a residual American role in the region as a counterbalance to what is seen as an increasingly xenophobic and anti-Islamic Europe. Europe's arm's length attitude to the current situation in Algeria also disturbs the leadership, which is keen to give the impression of "business as usual" in Algiers.[14]

In the past, and most notably following the serious anti-government riots of 1988, Algeria has sought the active participation of France and other European countries in efforts to promote economic development and alleviate popular frustration with FLN rule.[15] The current political turmoil, coupled with a growing disinclination in Algiers to contemplate real economic reform, suggest a very gloomy outlook for foreign investment. The most attractive sector for economic cooperation on a north-south basis continues to be the natural gas industry.[16] Europe and the United States are leading markets for Algeria's hydrocarbon exports (these account for 95 percent of the country's total export revenues), and the planned construction of a new high-capacity gas pipeline to bring Algerian gas to Europe via Morocco and Gibraltar will increase the country's energy "reach." Although oil production has been steadily declining, Algeria possesses the world's seventh largest reserves of natural gas; it is the third largest supplier to the EC, behind Norway and the former Soviet Union. The eventual development of Trieste as an economic gateway to eastern and central Europe would provide another natural outlet for Algerian gas, augmenting the existing Transmed pipeline to Italy.[17] The primacy of gas exports for Algeria's economic well-being suggests that a "radical" Islamic regime in Algiers would find it difficult to dismantle the existing web of relations with the West even if it wished to do so.[18] In the same vein, regional adventurism and the prospect of conflict with Morocco or Libya would pose a serious

---

[14]See Alan Riding, "France Voices Concern over Situation in Algeria," *New York Times,* January 14, 1992; "Mitterrand on Consequences of Algerian Crisis," *FBIS-West Europe Report,* January 15, 1992, p. 15; and "European Parliament Puts Algerian Aid on Hold," *FBIS-West Europe Report,* January 17, 1992, p. 1.

[15]One hundred sixty people are reported to have been killed during the "Black October" riots of October 6–11, 1988. *North Africa: Economic Structure and Analysis (EIU),* p. 46. For an assessment of the 1988 riots in terms of Algeria's history, see Alfred Sherman, "Algeria—An Intellectual Fashion Revisited," *The World Today,* January 1989.

[16]See James Audu, "Oil: Algeria's Engine of Development," *OPEC Bulletin,* January 1990.

[17]"Imports of Algerian Gas, Petroleum Discussed," *Mondo Economico* (Milan), in *FBIS-West Europe Report,* February 19, 1992, p. 8.

[18]Mortimer, *European Security After the Cold War, op. cit.,* p. 38.

risk of interruption in Algeria's gas production and exports—a further disincentive to radicalism.

REGIONAL INTEGRATION

Algeria regards itself as the natural center of gravity in the Maghreb and the natural leader of efforts toward regional integration. The Algerian presidency of the AMU in the second half of 1990 was a period of particularly intense activity with agreements on the establishment of a customs union and other accords aimed at the development of an integrated market. To date, very little has been accomplished in the way of implementation.[19] Above all, and from the Algerian perspective, the AMU has been a useful vehicle for regional activism at a time when such traditional outlets as the nonaligned movement are in decline. More tangibly, the AMU framework has offered a graceful way of disengaging from the western Sahara dispute and improving relations with Morocco. To the extent that moves toward regional integration, whether symbolic or substantive, can give the Maghreb countries greater influence in dealing with the EC and the wealthy states of the Gulf, Algiers will benefit. The combination of the Gulf crisis, the Libyan embargo, and the mounting turmoil in Algiers has left the AMU in limbo. In any case, the Algerian leadership cannot be expected to focus on regional integration unless and until the internal security situation is stabilized.

DEFENSE POLICY

Since the revolution, the armed forces have been a central pillar of the Algerian regime, a position threatened by the political reforms after 1988 but reasserted strongly in the wake of the military-backed coup of 1991. Current Defense Minister Khaled Nezzar is in a position of *de facto* national leadership. Internal security concerns dominate the defense agenda, and the battle against Islamic extremists is now the overwhelming mission of the security forces.[20] The

---

[19]On the prospects for economic implementation, in particular, the potential complementarity (or lack of complementarity) among the Maghrebi economies, see Zallio, *op. cit.*, pp. 55–59.

[20]These forces have been strengthened substantially over the past year with the addition of 13,000 men and the formation of a new paramilitary National Security

military has arrested a process under which the political power of Islamic groups was steadily increasing but at significant cost to Algerian society and, potentially, its own cohesion should the ranks of FIS sympathizers within the armed forces expand.[21]

Over the last decade, the Algerian armed forces have undergone a progressive movement away from a "people's army" and toward a more professional organization capable of operating modern equipment and conducting modern warfare.[22] The bulk of the Algerian military hardware was supplied by the Soviet Union, with whom the Algerian armed forces maintained significant professional and technical contact. Soviet advisors and technicians have had a substantial presence in Algeria since the 1960s. Even in the wake of the breakup of the Soviet Union, and as late as the spring of 1992, as many as 300 ex-Soviet advisors remained in the country, including some of general officer rank.

Algeria is interested in diversifying its sources of military hardware, particularly in the wake of the Soviet collapse.[23] But the country's current economic crisis and depressed hydrocarbon revenues suggest a renewed effort to purchase easily integrated hardware from ex-Soviet stocks at low cost. Apart from a keen interest in acquiring spares for the large inventory of Soviet tanks, helicopters, and aircraft, the Algerian military is likely to seek more advanced aircraft (e.g., MiG-29s) as a counter to the Moroccan purchase of 20 F-16s. The Algerian Navy operates two Kilo-class submarines along with two Romeo-class boats for training. Algeria may seek to buy additional Kilo-class diesel submarines from Russia, a development that would reinforce submarine proliferation trends in the Third World.[24]

Force (16,000 men), a Republican Guard Brigade, and an augmented Gendarmerie, all lightly equipped. New coastal patrol craft have been purchased as part of a campaign against gun running. The army as a whole is being reorganized on a divisional basis; four divisions total, two armored, two mechanized. IISS, *Military Balance*, 1992–1993.

[21]See Remy Leveau, *Algeria: Adversaries in Search of Uncertain Compromises* (Paris: WEU Institute for Security Studies, Chaillet Paper No. 4, September 1992).

[22]EIU, p. 48. Total active strength in 1992 was 139,000 (84,000 conscripts), 150,000 army reserves.

[23]One possibility would be the purchase of Italian or Spanish equipment in exchange for natural gas.

[24]On the pattern of reported Iranian purchases from Russia, see Slade, *op. cit.*

NUCLEAR AND MISSILE PROGRAMS: A SEARCH FOR STRATEGIC WEIGHT?

Algeria's nuclear program has been the subject of considerable spec-ulation among Western observers. Taken together with allegations that Algeria is exploring the purchase of Korean and Chinese ballistic missiles, the nuclear issue (coupled with the possibility of an Islamic political triumph) has taken center stage in the debate over Algeria's post-Cold War role. Algerian policymakers are well aware of the sensitivity of the nuclear question in the context of relations with Europe and the United States, particularly in the wake of the Gulf conflict. The Algerian leadership regards the nuclear program as closely tied to the country's international prestige and regional influ-ence. As one leading Algerian observer and former high-ranking of-ficial asserts: "In ten years time there will be two countries in Africa which are taken seriously by the U.S.—South Africa and Algeria; both will be nuclear powers." It is difficult to know what weight to attach to this. The comment was intended to stress the significance of Algeria's civil nuclear program for the country's development and prestige, but the potential strategic implications cannot be ignored

Since the establishment of a nuclear development program in 1983, Algeria has acquired two reactors, both ostensibly for civilian pur-poses. The first is a small (one megawatt) research reactor at Draria outside Algiers. The second reactor, under construction at Ain Oussera 270 km south of Algiers, was not openly acknowledged until 1991 and has been the subject of intense speculation in the West.[25] The Ain Ouserra reactor, built by China, is nominally rated at 15 MW, but is potentially of 40 MW capacity—sufficiently powerful to pro-duce plutonium for a nuclear weapons program. Chinese nuclear technicians have taken up residence in considerable numbers. Algeria has placed the experimental reactor at Draria under IAEA safeguards and has agreed to the presence of inspectors at Ain Ouserra once the reactor is completed. Algeria is not a signatory of

---

[25]Numerous accounts appeared in the *Times* (London), the *Washington Post,* and the *Washington Times* in 1991, all based on reputed intelligence "leaks." The expulsion of the British military attache, allegedly for taking photographs at the site, only served to heighten speculation about the plant. See LaFranchi, *op. cit.*

the Non-Proliferation Treaty, but has said that it intends to join.[26] Algeria has strongly defended the claim that its nuclear program is strictly for civilian purposes, principally electric power generation (despite the absence of a generating plant and transmission equipment).[27]

More disturbing are reports that Algeria is cooperating with Iraq to provide a sanctuary for Iraqi nuclear materials and technicians and may be pursuing a joint nuclear weapons program.[28] Regardless of the accuracy of these reports, a "nuclear axis" between Algeria, Iraq, or another Arab power would pose significant risks. Uranium and other special materials might be held in trust to avoid international scrutiny or until sufficient technical expertise can be assembled in Algeria. A more proximate risk would be the use of Iraqi uranium to breed plutonium in the Ain Oussera reactor.

The view that Algeria is contributing to the general level of Arab technological development is common in nationalist circles in Algiers. Equally pervasive is the concern that Algeria could become the victim of a preemptive western strike aimed at eliminating the country's nuclear program, on the pattern of operations against Iraq, and potentially against Libya. Above all, and perhaps this argues for the guarded approach of Algerian officials toward the matter, the possession of even a civilian nuclear program is a ready means of promoting Algeria's power and prestige. In short, it provides a substantial boost to Algeria's strategic weight in the eyes of regional actors such as Libya, Tunisia, and Morocco and in the eyes of the West. The risk that Algeria might opt for a weapons program might be compounded by the advent of an Islamic regime in Algiers, a deterioration of relations with Morocco, a crisis along north-south lines in the Mediterranean, or, most dangerously, a confluence of these developments.

---

[26]See Snyder, *op. cit.*, p. 89. See also Leonard S. Middle, "Threats in the Middle East," *Orbis*, Spring 1992, p. 190. Morocco, Tunisia, and Libya are signatories of the Non-Proliferation Treaty.

[27]Algeria would not be the first energy-rich state to opt for nuclear power, but its plentiful natural gas resources tend to raise certain suspicions.

[28]"Saddam Helps Algeria Make Islamic Nuclear Bomb," *Sunday Times* (London), January 5, 1992; "Algeria and the Bomb," *The Economist*, January 11, 1992; and Youssef Ibrahim, "Algeria Offers Atom Arms Vow," *New York Times*, January 8, 1992.

A more proximate risk to regional stability and the security of southern Europe is posed by Algeria's potential acquisition of ballistic missiles capable of reaching population centers and military facilities across its borders and across the Mediterranean. Libya is reported to have begun negotiations with North Korea for the purchase of Scud-C (600 km) missiles, as well as the 1000 km No-Dong 1, a Scud-C derivative.[29] Algeria will be in a position to acquire similar systems from Korea or China should the government wish to spend the necessary hard currency. The desire for regional leverage and geopolitical weight that provides much of the motivation for Algeria's nuclear program is likely to produce a similar and more easily satisfied demand for ballistic missiles. If states elsewhere in the Arab world continue to acquire these systems, and go further to develop the capability for their manufacture, the incentives for Algeria to follow suit will be very strong.

REGIONAL SECURITY CONCERNS

Algeria's external security concerns have largely receded as the government and the military have become absorbed in the repression of the Islamic opposition. Nonetheless, Algeria has a long-standing concern about Moroccan regional ambitions. Morocco and Algeria have clashed in the past over territorial issues in the Sahara, and military and political support for the Polisario Front in its struggle for control of the western Sahara has until recently been a central strand of Algeria's regional competition with Morocco. The competition with Morocco and support for the Polisario was also part of a broader competition between superpower patrons. The end of the Cold War and the disappearance of the Soviet Union from the scene combined with financial and political crisis to force a reassessment of Algerian policy toward the western Sahara. Algiers has dropped its costly support for the Polisario and has pursued a policy of detente with Rabat, leaving the field clear for a settlement of the Sahara dispute on Moroccan terms. Stabilization of the internal situation in Algeria, or the victory of Islamist forces, might produce a regime in Algiers with the ability and inclination for an active policy toward the Sahara question. Over the longer term, the geopolitical competition with

---

[29]*Middle East Defense News,* May 18, 1992; Seib, *op. cit.*

Morocco could reassert itself strongly, not least if Algiers fears the creation of a "greater Morocco" incorporating the western Sahara.

A militant Islamic victory in Algeria would place great pressure on Morocco and Tunisia. The prospect of Islamic insurgents operating against Rabat from bases in Algeria could well prove a *casus belli* for King Hassan or his successor. Moroccan control over the planned gas pipeline from Algeria to Spain could also prove a cause of conflict against a background of regional tension, but Morocco would have little incentive to interfere with a lucrative arrangement short of a major crisis. The pipeline is more likely to encourage a confluence of regional interests.[30]

On a secondary level, Algerians are concerned about the consequences of Libyan unpredictability and adventurism. As elsewhere in the Maghreb, the Libyan people are well liked, but Qaddafi is viewed as a wild card and a regional embarrassment. Despite concerns over Libyan intervention in Chad, the potential for a Libyan-Algerian confrontation is low (an Islamic regime that sought to export its revolution to Tripoli would transform this situation). A more serious concern is that Qaddafi's adventurism will provoke a new crisis with the West in which Algerian public opinion will rally behind a brother Arab state, posing more dangerous dilemmas on the pattern of the Gulf War.

Algerian officials are concerned about the availability of outside support for extremist factions within the Islamic movement, although this would be less an external challenge than an extension of the internal struggle against the FIS. Beyond Saudi financial support for the FIS, there is a fear that Iran may become seriously involved in the Islamic insurgency. The advent of an Islamic government in the Sudan with close ties to Teheran is viewed with alarm, both as a political precedent and as a possible conduit for arms and other assistance to groups within Algeria.

There has been a sharp increase in incidents of banditry, including the kidnapping and murder of European tourists by Tuareg tribesman in the region south of Tamanraset. The limited ability of

---

[30]"Agreement with Algeria for Gas Pipeline Signed," *FBIS-West Europe Report,* May 1, 1991, p. 19.

the Algerian military to fully control the vast territory in the south of the country is an additional issue of concern to the government. The military is interested in acquiring modern photographic and electronic intelligence equipment to assist in the maintenance of order in the south, and, more important, to monitor Moroccan activity along the border in the west.

Finally, looking beyond the Mediterranean shore, Algeria is aware of the potential for a preemptive U.S. or even Israeli strike against Algeria's nuclear or future ballistic missile sites, referred to earlier. A more radical regime in Algiers might well begin to view the possession of a minimum nuclear and ballistic missile capability, together with a more potent submarine force, as a useful deterrent in the absence of a superpower patron. Again, a general deterioration in north-south relations in the Mediterranean over such issues as immigration, religion, or developments elsewhere in the Middle East could reinforce the proliferation dynamic.

Algeria has supported the concept of CSCM (Conference on Security and Cooperation in the Mediterranean). Indeed, before the virtual complete absorption of the Algerian leadership in domestic problems, Algeria emerged as an enthusiastic supporter of a "global" CSCM, encompassing a vast area from Mauritania to the Persian Gulf, as originally proposed by Italy and Spain. The preferred approach from the Algerian perspective would emphasize cooperation on underlying political and economic problems, without a strong security component. Algeria has been less receptive to the alternative, French-sponsored approach centering on north-south cooperation in the western Mediterranean, but is a participant in the current "Five plus Five" negotiations along these lines. Once a leading proponent of naval arms control in the Mediterranean, Algeria now emphasizes the right of regional powers to develop adequate means of self defense, including the possession of unconventional weapons. Algerian analysts invariably point to Israel's conventional and unconventional arsenals as a justification for this stance.

PROSPECTS FOR BILATERAL RELATIONS WITH THE UNITED STATES

Despite American support for the principle of Algerian independence, which many Algerians remember and continue to cite as grounds for optimism on bilateral relations, and significant energy ties, the history of relations between Washington and Algiers since the revolution has been mixed at best. Algeria's activism in support of the nonaligned movement and close ties to radical Third World states unfolded against a background of East-West competition that made cool relations a virtual inevitability. Close U.S. ties to Morocco and Algeria's military ties to the Soviet Union and Eastern Europe (notably, Algeria never provided the Soviet Union with bases) reinforced the distance between Washington and Algiers.[31] Algerians, who take their country's reputation for activism in international affairs seriously, were particularly disturbed by the perceived failure of Washington to express adequate gratitude to Algeria for its efforts as an interlocutor in the negotiations over the fate of the U.S. hostages held in Iran and eventually released in Algiers in January 1981.[32]

In 1985, President Benjedid became the first Algerian head of state to visit Washington since independence in 1962. In the aftermath of the Cold War, and with a process of political and economic reform under way in Algeria, the way seemed open for closer bilateral relations. The abortive elections and the installation of an unstable military-led regime has made Algeria a difficult and unappealing partner for the United States in the Maghreb. The resumption of more active relations between Washington and Algiers will be difficult to contemplate until the domestic situation in Algeria is stabilized and a government with sufficient political legitimacy establishes itself. In the interim, the attitude of the United States and the West as a whole toward the Islamic movement in Algeria will be an important and potentially precedent setting example for relations between Islam and the West more broadly.

---

[31]Since 1986, the United States has had a small IMET (International Military Education and Training) program in Algeria, funded at $150 million in 1992, with matching funds from Algeria.

[32]Parker, *op. cit.*, p. 50.

Over the longer term, the United States will have a strong stake in developing positive relations with Algeria. First, Algeria is arguably the region's leading actor, with immense human and material resources, and substantial actual and potential military power. Second, the political, economic, and security fate of Morocco and Tunisia will depend to a large extent on the course of developments in Algeria. Third, Algeria is unlikely to abandon its tradition of international activism for long. It will remain an influential actor within the Arab world and within the Third World.[33] Finally, Algeria's proliferation potential, coupled with its likely search for strategic weight, suggests the importance of minimizing the Algerian sense of exposure to external challenges, not least the risk of a confrontation with the United States.

The current regime clearly wishes to develop a closer relationship with Washington as a means of diversifying its relations, including its arms supply relationships. At a time when many Algerians are concerned about the emergence of xenophobic, anti-Islamic trends along the northern shore of the Mediterranean, closer relations with the United States appear as an attractive balance to Europe. Would an Islamic regime in Algiers be amenable to positive relations with the United States and the West as a whole? A moderate Islamist regime, or a coalition government in which Islamic forces share power with secular parties, probably would. Even a more radical Islamic regime would find it difficult and counterproductive to dismantle the extensive network of political and economic ties with the West. As in Iran, the imperatives of an energy-based economy will make themselves felt. But unlike Iran, Algeria is less than 200 miles from Europe, with all that this implies for access to European media and the consequences for public opinion. In the worst case, the advent of a radical Islamic regime with active international ambitions risks the creation of another and more potent pariah state in the Maghreb—closer to Iran than Libya in terms of its regional power and potential.

Algeria is likely to loom increasingly large in U.S. strategy toward the Mediterranean basin. But the potential for deeper bilateral relations

---

[33]These arguments for a more active U.S. policy toward Algeria are developed in Entelis, *op. cit.*

on many fronts cannot be realized without a resumption of the democratic process in Algeria. Establishing closer ties with the current military-backed regime is unlikely to improve the long-term outlook for relations as the legitimacy of the old FLN-inspired order continues to decline. U.S. policy should be firmly and unambiguously oriented toward the promotion of democracy in Algeria. Future economic and security assistance initiatives should be made contingent on progress in this direction.

Chapter Five

TUNISIA

A CONSUMER OF SECURITY

As a small and relatively affluent state sandwiched between Algeria and Libya, and with a negligible capacity for self defense and an active internal security problem, Tunisia is the Maghreb's leading "consumer" of security. The country's delicate internal and external situation gives rise to competing foreign and security policy objectives. On the one hand, Tunis has a clear interest in maintaining close relations with its leading security guarantors in the West and close economic relations with the EC. On the other hand, the strength of pro-Arab, anti-Western opinion in periods of crisis such as the Gulf War cannot be ignored by the political elite. These tensions in Tunisian policy will continue and perhaps deepen, with significant implications for the stability of the regime and relations with the West.

Tunisia is in many ways the most thoroughly Westernized and developed country in the Maghreb. The society has been relatively relaxed about retaining its French cultural heritage.[1] Over the course of President Bourguiba's long tenure as head of the Destourian (Constitutionalist) Party from 1956–1987, and under the leadership of his successor, Ben Ali, who seized power in a bloodless coup, Tunisia has pursued a generally pro-Western course in international

---

[1]David C. Gordon, *Images of the West: Third World Perspectives* (Savage: Rowman and Littlefield, 1989), p. 138.

affairs.[2]   Like his contemporaries in Algeria, Bourguiba played an active role within the Arab world and the nonaligned movement, but the thrust of Tunisian policy was Western-looking and avowedly secular, emphasizing the country's role as an interlocutor between north and south.   To a degree, this was a natural outgrowth of Tunisia's long history as a cultural, commercial, and strategic entrepot at the center of the Mediterranean.   Indeed, in many respects, Tunisia is the most tangibly Mediterranean country in the region.   Without in any sense abandoning the country's ties to the West, the Ben Ali government has adopted a more diversified approach, giving greater weight to Tunisia's African, Arab, and Maghrebi vocations.[3]

Ben Ali's approach is shared only to a degree by the political and economic elite, most of whom view Tunisia's future as inextricably tied to the evolution of relations with the EC.   Indeed, many members of the elite describe Tunisia as a political, economic, and strategic extension of Europe.[4]   From this perspective, the radicalizing effect of the Gulf War on Tunisian public opinion and the continuing pattern of fundamentalist challenge and government repression have been disastrous for Tunisia's ambitions as they relate to Europe. These factors will only reinforce the diversion of European aid, investment, and political attention from south to east, to the detriment of Tunisia.

THE CHALLENGE OF RADICAL ISLAM

The prospective diversion of Western attention eastward could not come at a more inconvenient time for Tunisia. As elsewhere in the Maghreb, economic development is seen as the solution to the underlying demographic and social problems fueling the Islamic op-

---

[2]See L. B. Ware, "Ben Ali's Constitutional Coup in Tunisia," *Middle East Journal,* Autumn 1988; and Dirk Vandewalle, "From the New State to the New Era: Toward a Second Republic in Tunisia," *Middle East Journal,* Autumn 1988.

[3]See Anne Joyce, "Interview: Zine El Abidine Ben Ali," *American-Arab Affairs,* Fall 1989.

[4]These views are strikingly similar to those found in Turkey; there is an extensive pattern of commercial and diplomatic contacts between the two countries.

position movements.[5] Unlike its Maghrebi neighbors, Tunisia may be in the best position to make significant progress in this area within a politically relevant span of time.[6] The distributional inequalities in Tunisia are less pronounced than in Morocco, and the scale of the economic challenge is less immense. Rigid bureaucracy and state dirigisme continue to hamper efforts at economic reform and discourage foreign investors.   Nonetheless, the extent of Tunisia's interdependence with Europe (75 percent of trade is with the EC, only 9 percent with Maghreb neighbors), its proximity, and its labor surplus have encouraged a pattern of European manufacturing in Tunisia for reexport to the continental market.

Even Tunisia's active, export-driven economy has been unable to provide jobs for a vast number of young and politically aware Tunisians. Roughly 370,000 of the country's total workforce of 2.4 million are unemployed. The result has been growing social strain and migration pressure in a country that had been a net importer of labor until the 1960s. Some 500,000 Tunisians work abroad, half in France. As the EC places mounting restrictions on legal immigration, there is a growing sense of public frustration and elite concern about the loss of an important safety valve.[7]

The Ben Ali regime faces a strong challenge from the various factions of the Islamic En Nadha (Renaissance) Movement, the largest of which is led by Rachid Ghannouchi.[8] The movement has been banned and its members driven underground in the face of a sweeping campaign of government repression. The number of En Nadha sympathizers arrested over the last two years is put at 7,000 by Western observers and 30,000 by En Nadha spokesmen. In a recent trial of nearly 300 fundamentalists accused of plotting the armed

---

[5]Elbaki Hermassi, "L'Etat Tunisien et le Mouvement Islamiste," *Annuaire de l'Afrique du Nord*, xxviii, 1989. See also Lisa Anderson, "Obligation and Accountability: Islamic Politics in North Africa," *Daedalus*, Summer 1991.

[6]A useful Tunisian perspective on the evolution and future of the Tunisian economy can be found in Hachemi Alaya, *L'Economie Tunisienne* (Tunis: Afkar et Ich'har, 1989).

[7]Alan Cowell, "Tunis Journal: In a Jobless Land, the Way Up Means a Visa Out," *New York Times*, July 7, 1992.

[8]Ghannouchi, a university professor, has sought political asylum in Britain, having been expelled by the Algerian government at the request of Tunisia. For a time he was reported to be living in the Sudan.

overthrow of the state and the establishment of an Islamic regime, 250 were sentenced to prison, 50 for life.[9] The scale and severity of the crackdown has raised human rights concerns in Europe and the United States. Tunisia's own Human Rights League, a leading forum for dissent, has been dissolved.[10]

Tunisia has been at the forefront of efforts to develop a Maghreb-wide campaign against the militant Islamic movements, arguing for heightened cooperation to close avenues of external support for En Nadha, Algeria's FIS, and other groups. Tunisian observers have pointed to the growing role of Iran and the Sudan in providing financial and material support for Islamic militants who move across borders relatively unimpeded.[11] Weapons may also be smuggled into Algeria and Tunisia via Chad, Niger, and the Tuareg tribes in Mali. A certain amount of gun-running probably occurs along the Mediterranean coast. Much of the armament probably comes from raided military and police depots in Algeria. As the situation within Algeria has deteriorated, Tunisian officials have come to fear the advent of an Islamic regime in Algiers bent on exporting its revolution to the east and west. The problem of internal stability and the suppression of En Nadha absorbs most of Tunisia's limited security resources. Under these circumstances, external risks have assumed a secondary place on the agenda of the Ben Ali regime.

THE GULF EXPERIENCE AND THE POWER OF PUBLIC OPINION

The tension between the elite's moderate, Western orientation and public perceptions was dramatically illustrated by Tunisia's stance during the Gulf War. The Ben Ali government, against the background of widespread public support for Saddam Hussein and the government's own experimentation with a more Arab-oriented for-

---

[9]Youssef Ibrahim, "Tunisia Puts Nearly 300 Muslim Militants on Trial," *New York Times*, August 3, 1992; *The Economist*, September 12, 1992, p. 44.

[10]Tod Robberson, "Tunisia Accused of Torturing Political Prisoners: Amnesty International Report Cites Crackdown on Islamic Fundamentalist Opposition," *Washington Post*, March 4, 1992.

[11]Youssef Ibrahim, "Algeria and Tunisia Intensify Anti-Fundamentalist Efforts," *New York Times*, December 19, 1991.

eign policy, adopted a critical attitude toward the coalition operations against Iraq. The respected Foreign Minister, Ismail Khalil, was abruptly replace by Harib Boulares, a close associate of the president, apparently as a result of Khalil's reluctance to carry forward what he regarded as an anti-Western policy.[12] The pressure of public opinion clearly dictated a policy of rhetorical support for the Iraqi position, while quietly complying with UN imposed sanctions on Baghdad. But even rhetorical support imposed and continues to impose costs on the Tunisian regime. Kuwait, for example, has made it clear that it will not entertain future Tunisian requests for aid.[13] Western officials, taken aback by the character and virulence of the Tunisian stance, remain wary, although relations are steadily returning to normal across the board. On the whole, the Tunisian elite, not least the Foreign Ministry, regards the episode as a tactically inevitable embarrassment.

The Gulf experience points to the continuing challenge for the Tunisian regime of accommodating volatile public opinion while pursuing closer economic and strategic ties with the West and especially the United States. Public sentiment could play an important role in future crises involving Libya or Algeria. It would be unreasonable to expect the Tunisian regime to run the considerable internal risk of openly supporting Western action against either country (e.g., in the context of counter-proliferation or as a response to state-sponsored terrorism) unless Tunisia itself was threatened. The problems posed for the regime in the conduct of its foreign and security policy are substantial, and all the more serious as Tunisia seeks to develop a new basis for relations with the West after the Cold War.

---

[12]George Joffe, "North African Responses to the Gulf Crisis," in EIU, *North Africa*, p. 6.

[13]*Ibid.*, p. 8. Western observers have also speculated on the extent to which Ben Ali's displeasure with Saudi support for fundamentalist groups within Tunisia may have suggested a pro-Iraqi stance. Fundamentalist groups in Tunisia and Algeria did not openly support the Iraqi position, reportedly out of deference to their Saudi sponsors. Anderson, *op. cit.*, p. 109.

NORTH-SOUTH RELATIONS

Tunisia is finding it increasingly difficult to reconcile hopes for an ever-closer economic and political relationship with Europe with evidence of growing xenophobia and anti-North African sentiment across the continent. The mistreatment of Tunisian immigrants in France and Italy is a common topic in the Tunisian press. The fear of being held at arm's length by Europe, or worse, becoming an object of hostility, is as tangible in Tunisia as elsewhere in the Maghreb. A more subtle concern for some Tunisian intellectuals is that the pressure for Western-style democratization will upset the political order in Tunisia without bringing the economic progress necessary for stability. They fear that the West will push for democracy but prove unwilling to provide economic assistance and investment. Others presumably hope that the West will do more to encourage the liberalization of Tunisian politics.

Tunis is a participant in cooperative initiatives in the western Mediterranean, notably the "Five plus Five" arrangement.[14] Officials have expressed their disappointment with the lack of progress in this forum, largely as a result of the Lockerbie dispute.[15] The government would support the renewal of the CSCM initiative for Mediterranean cooperation on security, broadly defined. Tunisia has a greater stake than most in arrangements such as CSCE and CSCM, which take as their starting point respect for existing borders. The current regime might be less comfortable with the proposed human rights "basket." Tunis would be most sensitive to the treatment of the Palestinian issue within the CSCM framework (Tunisia has a long history of involvement in Palestinian affairs and the PLO is based in Tunis).

Tunisia stands to lose a great deal as a result of heightened tension between north and south in the Mediterranean. Its economic and political development would be retarded, and its importance as an interlocutor between Europe, the Maghreb, and the Arab world would decline to the extent that security issues come to the fore. Tunisia's importance is largely commercial and diplomatic. A north-

---

[14]"Charter Signed with Tunisia, France, Spain, Italy," Rabat MAP, in *FBIS-NES*, 28 September 1992. See also Joyce, *op. cit.*

[15]Azouz Ennifar, "The Threat to Stability in the Mediterranean Region: A Tunisian Perspective," in O'Brien, *op. cit.*, p. 174.

south military confrontation in the Mediterranean would place Tunisia at the mercy of developments led by Rabat, Tripoli, or Algiers.

REGIONAL INTEGRATION

Tunisia has supported AMU attempts to encourage regional economic integration, but few observers are enthusiastic about the prospects for what many consider a platform for Moroccan and Algerian activism.[16] There is a perception that Rabat will be the least willing to compromise on questions of national sovereignty. Above all, Tunisia's attitude toward the AMU is colored by the overwhelming weight of economic relations with Europe. A more favorable bilateral arrangement with the EC would be infinitely preferable to the dim prospect of Maghrebi unity. From a security perspective, however, Tunisia does have a strong interest in anchoring Algeria and Libya within a broader Maghrebi institution.

EXTERNAL SECURITY CONCERNS

Tunisia has only a small military establishment and devotes a far lower percentage of its GNP to defense than either of its Maghrebi neighbors.[17] Tunisian strategy accepts as a given the impossibility of conducting more than an initial defense of its borders and relies on the prospect of friendly intervention from the United States, Europe, or elsewhere in the Maghreb. Algeria, Libya, and Israel are the leading sources of external risk as seen by the Tunisian foreign and security policy elite. To a greater or lesser degree, all three sources of risk incorporate an internal as well as an external dimension.

Tunisia has traditionally been uneasy about Algerian intentions in the region. The sheer size and military potential of its western neighbor, coupled with Algeria's reputation for activism and the espousal of a brand of Arab socialism at odds with the more moderate

---

[16]The current secretary of the AMU is a Tunisian.

[17]The Tunisian armed forces consist of 35,000 men, 26,000 of whom are conscripts. The total 1992 defense budget was no more than $500 million, although this may not fully reflect resources devoted to internal security. The air force totals 38 combat aircraft, including 15 F-5E/F.

ideology in Tunis, have tended to make Tunisians uneasy. Algerian officials were suspected of complicity in the 1980 Gafsa raid (see below) in which Libyan-trained insurgents entered the country from Algeria. In the wake of the Gafsa incident, relations with Algeria have steadily improved. A Treaty of Friendship and Cooperation signed between the two countries in 1983 has led to a significant degree of cooperation on security matters, and Algeria has emerged as a possible guarantor of Tunisian security in the event of a Libyan attack.[18] The escalating confrontation between Islamist and government forces in Algeria has, however, once again made Algeria a leading source of risk for Tunisia. Tunisians are not sanguine about the prospects for a quick return to stability in Algiers. There is serious concern that prevailing conditions in Algeria will continue to encourage Islamic activists in Tunisia and elsewhere in the Maghreb. The advent of an Islamic regime in Algeria would pose the threat of an "Islamic axis" stretching from the Sudan to Algeria and perhaps Morocco.[19]

If one discounts the serious implications for Tunisia's domestic stability of an Islamic victory in Algiers, Libya is by far the most prominent source of external risk. In January 1980, 50–60 dissident Tunisians armed and trained in Libya attacked the police and army barracks in the Tunisian town of Gafsa. The aim was apparently to spark an uprising against the Bourghiba government. The operation was defeated by Tunisian forces after heavy fighting and the loss of 40 lives. Notably, France was the first of Tunisia's allies to respond, sending a small naval force to the coast.[20] Tensions flared again in 1985 when Libya expelled roughly a third of the Tunisian workers in the country and concentrated troops on the border. Such incidents (the most recent of which was another round of worker expulsions in September 1992), against the background of Libyan radicalism and the concentration of ex-Soviet military equipment across the border,

---

[18]Maurizio Cremasco, "Two Uncertain Futures: Tunisia and Libya," in *Prospects for Security in the Mediterranean, Part III*, p. 47. See also Frederick Ehrenreich, "National Security" in *Tunisia: A Country Study* (Washington, D.C.: Department of the Army, 1988); and Marquina, *op. cit.*, p. 33.

[19]Tunisia has accused the Sudan of operating training camps used by the En Nadha movement. "Terror Threat from Sudan Worries West," *Middle East Defense News*, December 23, 1991.

[20]Parker, *op. cit.*, p. 171.

have served to keep the Libyan threat at the forefront of Tunisian concerns.[21] The potential for a confrontation with Libya has also given substance to Tunisian security relationships with the West, above all the United States and France.

Although far from the center of the Arab-Israeli dispute, Tunisia is perhaps the most sensitive of all the Maghrebi countries to developments in the Levant and the implications for the country's security. Tunisian commentators inevitably cite the Palestinian issue as the leading source of risk in the Mediterranean region, and attitudes toward the problem exert a significant influence on the style if not the substance of Tunisia's relations with the West and the Arab world. Much of this concern stems from the Israeli air attack on the PLO's headquarters at Hamman-Lif outside of Tunis on October 1, 1985. At least 20 Tunisians were killed in the raid. The attack also confirmed the privately held view of many in the Tunisian elite that the PLO's presence in the country is a liability. Tunisian territory is placed at risk, domestic stability is not improved, and Western countries are made uneasy by the PLO presence. A Middle East settlement that addresses the Palestinian issue would contribute enormously to the perception of security in Tunis.

Finally, the issue of proliferation, and the chemical, nuclear, and ballistic missile programs under way in Algeria and Libya, have just begun to emerge as a concern in political and military circles. Military planners are clearly disturbed by the implications of proliferation, both for the regional military balance and, as important, for the behavior of the United States and Europe. On this as on other matters, opinion reflects the tension between strategic concerns and popular politics. Tunisian observers are worried by the possibility that the West will be deterred from intervening against an attack on Tunisia *but* also concerned that the United States will intervene preemptively to prevent the deployment of weapons of mass destruction. At the same time, many Tunisians point to the "double standard" employed by the West in condemning "technological progress" in the Arab world while ignoring long-standing Israeli programs.

---

[21]"Al Qaddafi Willing to Meet West's Demands," *FBIS-NES*, September 30, 1992, p. 16.

PROSPECTS FOR BILATERAL RELATIONS

Tunisia's strategic significance has flowed from its vulnerability—its role as a leading consumer of security in the region—and its ability to exert a moderating influence on policy in the Maghreb and throughout the Arab world. Tunis has also played an important role as an interlocutor between north and south in the Mediterranean. To the extent that Libya remains an unpredictable actor and source of risk, the possibility of a clash with Tunisia will persist. In the event, the United States may find it necessary to intervene, presumably alongside France and possibly Italy, to prevent the country from being overrun. The incentives for Western intervention would be considerable: to uphold the principle of the inviolability of existing borders; to check Libyan adventurism; and to prevent Libya from placing ballistic missiles closer to southern European territory (the appendix map suggests the significant gain in coverage that would result from placing Libyan launchers on the Tunisian coast). Should a radical regime take power in Algiers, Tunisia would face new risks from this quarter. With regard to Libya and Algeria, the threats to Tunisian security are both internal and external.

There has not been any fundamental change in the Tunisian government's approach to defense policy; it continues to rely on external ties rather than indigenous military capability to insure against regional risks. The current level of foreign military assistance (roughly $14 million from all sources) is certainly inadequate to support an expansion of Tunisia's diminutive force structure. There will undoubtedly be continuing interest in modest purchases of advanced systems from the United States, possibly financed by Saudi Arabia if relations strained by the Gulf experience can be sufficiently repaired. Given the primacy of internal stability for security in Tunisia, the current IMET program probably represents a more important aspect of bilateral security cooperation. Over 2,000 military students have been sent to the United States under this program since 1968, including President Ben Ali.[22] The Tunisian Navy has begun to participate in naval and amphibious exercises with the Sixth Fleet. The desire to repair the damage done to bilateral relations as a result of Tunisia's pro-Iraqi stance during the Gulf War was

---

[22]"Tunisia: A Tradition of Openness," *The DISAM Journal*, Summer 1992.

clearly demonstrated during National Defense Minister Ben Dhia's visit to Washington in June 1992.[23]

As in Algiers, there has been a progressive movement away from the concept of "the Mediterranean for the Mediterraneans," which had reached its peak with the deployment of U.S. cruise missiles at Comiso on Sicily, toward a more pragmatic stance. The U.S. naval and air presence in the region is now more often described as a positive contribution to deterrence, of particular value in relation to Libya. The Tunisian military favors the maintenance of a U.S. land-based tactical air presence in the Mediterranean region but would prefer to see it based in southern Europe. A presence in Morocco, the subject of some speculation following the announcement of the withdrawal of the 401st Tactical Fighter Wing from Torrejon in Spain, would raise regional balance and political acceptance concerns in Tunis and Algiers.

Nonetheless, public opinion will continue to place limits on the character and, above all, the visibility of bilateral cooperation in the security sphere. Closer defense ties cannot alter the fundamental unpredictability of Tunisian policy in the context of future crises and could undermine the political position of the Ben Ali regime. Given a choice between opposition to Western initiatives and public wrath, the government will opt for self-preservation and choose the latter. On the other hand, Tunisian officials are most anxious to encourage economic ties, currently at a very modest level, as a useful means of diversifying the bilateral relationship.[24] Leading obstacles to closer relations, from the Tunisian perspective, include competing requirements for U.S. attention in Eastern Europe and the former Soviet Union, declining aid and security assistance budgets, and the perceived U.S. failure to distinguish between "moderate" Tunisia and the Arab world as a whole. Above all, Tunisian officials stress Washington's "incorrect assessment" of the Islamic protest movement as a human rights issue rather than a security problem. Tunisia faces growing criticism on this score as a consequence of its

---

[23]"Defense Minister, Delegation on Visit to U.S.," *FBIS-NES*, June 5, 1992, p. 8.

[24]In 1992, the U.S. share of Tunisian imports and exports was less then 5 percent in each case. "Foreign Economic Trends and Their Implications for the U.S.: Tunisia" (Tunis: U.S. Embassy, 1992), p. 2.

crackdown on En Nadha and the suppression of dissidents. As in Morocco, the turmoil in Algeria has made the introduction of democratic reforms a more distant prospect. Overall, the question of human rights and democracy in Tunisia is likely to serve as an obstacle to expanded ties with the United States and the EC just as the regime looks to the West for assistance in addressing its substantial internal and external challenges.

Chapter Six

OVERALL OBSERVATIONS AND CONCLUSIONS

As Europe and the United States begin to focus on the security and security-related problems emanating from the southern shore of the Mediterranean, the world view of the Maghrebi countries themselves—principally Morocco, Algeria, and Tunisia—will have an important bearing on the prospects for north-south relations. The environment for the United States as a Mediterranean air and naval power, and as a political actor in the region, will be conditioned by national perceptions and strategic cultures on both sides of the Mediterranean. In a post-Cold War security environment characterized by regional risks, strategy toward North Africa is likely to be a more complex exercise. Moreover, as the Gulf crisis demonstrated, events beyond the Mediterranean basin can have a direct effect on the stability of the Maghreb and European and American security interests. The issue of theater interdependence has not evaporated with the end of East-West competition. The strategic importance of North Africa is increasing in relative terms, but its character and the weight of individual states across the region is also changing, with significant implications for U.S. policy.

REGIONAL TRENDS

Prevailing perceptions in Morocco, Algeria, and Tunisia reflect key trends affecting security across the region and attitudes toward Europe and the United States:

1. *The primacy of internal security.* For all of the countries surveyed, security is first and foremost domestic security. Without ignoring important regional rivalries and risks (e.g., Morocco-Algeria, Libya-

71

Tunisia), regimes are concerned above all with the maintenance of domestic stability. This is not a new development. But the growing strength of Islamic opposition movements across the region, together with growing pressure for democratization, have brought internal challenges to the forefront. All three countries face massive demographic and economic challenges of a long-term nature. As Europe tightens its restrictions on legal immigration, the ability of North African regimes to cope with the resulting social and political pressures will decline. The prospects for Western development assistance and investment on a scale sufficient to reverse these trends, and within a politically relevant timeframe, are slim. Competing demands for attention in the East, coupled with the EC's own development needs in southern Europe, worsen the outlook. When examined closely, many of the "external" threats to the security of states in the region are actually based in whole or in part on internal considerations and the perceived vulnerability of regimes to externally inspired rebellions.

2. *Militant Islam poses an immediate political challenge, with significant security implications.* Without exception, existing regimes in Rabat, Algiers, and Tunis regard the fundamentalist threat as an extraordinary challenge and are inclined to paint dire scenarios based on international links between extremist groups, Iranian and Sudanese backing, and the possibility of theocratic rule from Egypt to Mauritania. The advent of radical Islamic regimes in North Africa would undoubtedly have security consequences, not least because of the unpredictable interaction with such issues as migration and proliferation. But the emergence of an Islamist government through legitimate democratic means and the triumph of extremists as a result of violent struggle need not have the same consequences for European and American security interests. The principal risk from the Western perspective is that the Islamic opposition, having been forced out of the political process and driven underground, will come to be dominated by more extreme elements with more active international agendas. If the violent confrontation between the Algerian government and the FIS escalates, the prospects for a *modus vivendi* between north and south in the Mediterranean in security terms will worsen.

3. *North Africans fear a post-Cold War confrontation along north-south lines.* With the passing of the East-West competition, there is a

clear perception that a new ideological struggle is emerging between rich and poor, Islam and the West, north and south across the Mediterranean. In this context, Europe is the central focus of North African concern. The rise of xenophobic, anti-immigrant parties in Western and Eastern Europe, and the debate over the "threat from the south" in moderate foreign and security policy circles across Europe, have fueled these fears. The emergence of a functioning European defense capability would be of particular concern because of its presumed orientation toward "out-of-area" risks, including those emanating from the southern shore of the Mediterranean.

4. *The region as a whole will be characterized by a search for geostrategic weight after the Cold War.* Morocco, Algeria, and Tunisia are faced with a difficult problem of adjustment to post-Cold War realities. In Rabat and Tunis, pro-Western orientation and location astride critical maritime choke points are far less persuasive rationales for strategic attention in the absence of East-West competition. Algiers can no longer play one superpower against the other, and the nonaligned movement can no longer serve as an important vehicle for Algerian and Tunisian activism and a source of international prestige. In short, all three countries must embark on a search for geostrategic weight as a basis for "being taken seriously," both regionally and on the international scene. The means of achieving greater diplomatic and strategic weight could include regional integration through the AMU, closer bilateral relations with Europe or the United States, territorial extension, and the acquisition of weapons of mass destruction. As in the past, Algeria, Morocco, and Tunisia may also seek to further their prestige and influence through diplomatic mediation in international disputes.

5. *Incentives for proliferation are high; interest in arms control is low.* Algeria and Tunisia had been among the leading Cold War proponents of Mediterranean arms control, especially naval arms control, as a means of reducing the presence of the U.S. and the Soviet Union. In the post-Cold War environment, these countries have adopted a less-enthusiastic approach to regional arms control. The Gulf War experience has given impetus to the current view that states along the southern shore of the Mediterranean ought to enjoy the unrestricted ability to acquire the means of self defense, including the development of nuclear, chemical, ballistic missile, and submarine technology. The incentives for proliferation or "virtual" prolif-

eration (e.g., the Algerian nuclear program) are high in an era of diminished superpower influence over the behavior of regional actors, the fear of Western intervention, and the perceived double standard with regard to Israel's weapons programs. In broader terms, nuclear and ballistic missile programs—even the speculation associated with questionable initiatives such as the Ain Oussera reactor—are a potent source of strategic weight. Morocco and Tunisia pose low proliferation risks and should be concerned about the regional effects of Algerian or Libyan proliferation. Yet, outside a small circle of concerned military officials, criticism of proliferation trends in North Africa is muted.

6. *The region is characterized by a marked split between public and elite opinion, with strong implications for behavior in crises.* The Gulf War demonstrated the ability of public opinion to overwhelm even the most pro-Western governments. In a region where questions of internal stability are paramount, no regime will be willing to risk its own overthrow in support of Western aims in the Middle East or elsewhere. With the exception of threats to their own borders, crises within North Africa (e.g., a preemptive strike against Libya) would provoke at best an equivocal response, and at worst, outright opposition.

7. *Flashpoints for conflict in the region are largely, but not exclusively, south-south.* Leaving aside broader "milieu" conflicts over migration or trade, leading south-south flashpoints with a significant risk of the use of force include regional competition and territorial conflict between Algeria and Morocco, Libyan aggression against Tunisia, Moroccan or Tunisian conflict with Algeria over the activities of a revolutionary Islamic regime in Algiers, and renewed conflict in the Western Sahara, with or without Algerian or Libyan intervention. Only in the case of a Libyan or revolutionary Algerian move against Tunisia would there be a high probability of direct Western intervention.

Less likely, but with far greater consequences for European and U.S. security interests, are the following north-south flashpoints: a ballistic missile, nuclear, or chemical threat to European territory from Algeria or Libya; a Moroccan move against the Spanish enclaves of Ceuta and Melilla; an Algerian or Libyan attack on NATO ships or aircraft against the background of a major Middle Eastern or North

African crisis; a North African inspired terrorist incident or hostage crisis. Any of the above contingencies could lead to preemptive or retaliatory intervention.[1]

IMPLICATIONS FOR U.S. POLICY

U.S. interests in and policy toward North Africa and the Mediterranean region as a whole will be affected by the trends outlined above.

1. *Algeria is likely to emerge as the leading regional actor from the U.S. perspective.* Early restoration of the democratic process in Algeria holds the best chance of preventing the advent of a radical Islamic (or reactionary military) regime in Algiers. But regardless of the country's political evolution, Algeria's size, energy resources, penchant for international activism, military potential, and nuclear ambitions will make it a leading, probably *the* leading, actor in the region. Policy toward Algeria is likely to play a far more prominent role than in the past in U.S. strategy toward the region as a whole. An expansion of bilateral relations should be made conditional on clear progress toward democracy in Algeria.

2. *A high-profile presence or significantly expanded security cooperation with Morocco, Algeria, or Tunisia is neither possible nor desirable.* All three countries are keen to develop closer political, economic, and security assistance relations with the United States. With regard to more active security cooperation, or the provision of facilities on a permanent basis, only Morocco has expressed consistent interest. In the wake of the Gulf experience and its effect in North Africa, a high-profile presence or greatly expanded defense cooperation is inadvisable and probably impossible in any case. Expanded presence would pose unacceptable peacetime security risks for little strategic benefit (and presumably substantial cost). Political acceptance problems could prove corrosive of the legitimacy of existing regimes.

---

[1]The likely responses of individual southern European countries to such contingencies are assessed in Lesser, *op. cit.*

3. *The prospects for cooperation and access to facilities in times of crisis are poor (with some limited exceptions).* Again, in the wake of the Gulf experience, the prospects for predictable access to facilities and provision of overflight rights are poor with the exception of direct threats to the territorial integrity of Tunisia or Morocco. Even if access is granted, the open use of facilities to support operations elsewhere in the Arab world could have negative consequences for stability in the host country and in North Africa as a whole.

4. *The proliferation of weapons of mass destruction and the means for their delivery at increasing ranges will have a profound effect on security in southern Europe and will influence the prospects for cooperation in periods of crisis.* The ability of Algeria or Libya to hold at risk population centers (and U.S. and Allied military facilities) in southern Europe would exert a powerful influence on the security debate from Lisbon to Athens. The possibility, however remote, of retaliation against European territory will have a significant bearing on decisions about access, overflight, and active assistance in operations around the Mediterranean and beyond. This does not suggest that southern European countries will automatically shun cooperation with the United States in a future North African or Middle Eastern crisis for fear of becoming a target—far from it. What it does suggest is that southern European allies will expect a substantial measure of residual U.S. presence for the purposes of deterrence and reassurance in relation to contingencies outside the NATO area.[2]

5. The U.S. presence in and around the Mediterranean enjoys substantial support in Morocco and Tunisia; even in Algiers the United States is seen as a potentially valuable political counterbalance to Europe. As North Africans grow concerned about the future of relations with Europe on a variety of fronts, from immigration and trade to development assistance and security, improved relations with the United States loom as an attractive counterbalance and hedge in political, economic, and strategic terms. In more concrete terms, the U.S. presence in and around the Mediterranean is viewed by Rabat and Tunis as a critical contribution to their security in a more dangerous post-Cold War world.

---

[2]This theme is developed more thoroughly in Lesser, *op. cit.*

BALLISTIC MISSILE COVERAGE IN THE MEDITERRANEAN—CURRENT AND POTENTIAL

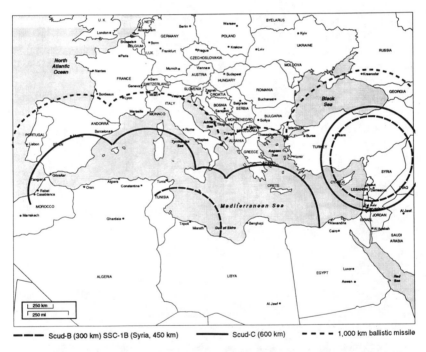

— — — Scud-B (300 km) SSC-1B (Syria, 450 km) ———— Scud-C (600 km) – – – 1,000 km ballistic missile

Figure A.1—The Geopolitics of Ballistic Missile Deployments in the Southern Mediterranean